"He's done it again! This book is an Encyclopedia of information that will put you in a position to close any situation, handle any objection and negotiate like a pro."

Ron Palmer, DCH Group

"Grant focuses on real world selling. A lot of people giving sales advice have never sold a thing in their life. Grant's techniques were forged in the real world and work in the real world. It's the best reference book on closing you'll ever see."

Duncan Scarry, Moore & Scarry Advertising

"This is your 'Bible' for closing and negotiating. No sales person should be without it!"

John Kostokos, Professional Sales Person

"G. Cardone shows you how to turn prospects and opportunities into deals and money."

Mimi Starrett, 20 Year Veteran of
Luxury Homes Sales in Beverly Hills

"The world is filled with sales people but what it is short on is professional closers. This book will make you a pro."

Michelle Seward, CEO of Protégé Financial

"In my 20 years in the business there has been no one that comes close to G. Cardone, don't just buy the book, buy them for all your salespeople as I did!"

Mark Hoch, Director of Sales

"Don't fool yourself into thinking you're a salesperson if you're not a closer. Selling without closing isn't selling at all. It's like being married without a spouse...impossible!"

C.P, CEO, Elan Vital LLC

"The information in this book is the most powerful and effective I have ever used!"

Steve Zakar, Retired Marine & Professional Sales Person

THE
GRANT CARDONE'S
REBUTTAL MANUAL
BOOK

How to close
anyone, anytime,
in any situation.

+

Over 100 ways
to ink the deal

"Learn to close, and you will never be without work, and will never be without money."

— *G. Cardone*

CONTENTS

THE GOAL
OF THIS BOOK

T he goal of this book is for you to become a master at the art of negotiating and closing transactions of any kind!

Learn to professionally handle any and all objections anywhere in the sales process. Whether it happens over the phone on a cold call or in the qualification, the negotiations, the close or the follow up.

Includes:

Over 100 Closes
205 Pages of High-Quality, Perfect Bound Real Life Responses
Amazing rebuttals and responses to everyday objections
You will master Grant Cardone's codification of how to close any sale by handling complaints and objections.

Drill on Grant Cardone's "Listen, acknowledge, isolate, validate, probe, tie down, justify and close" steps until you Perfect and Master the Objection.

Some of the objections The Grant Cardone Rebuttal Manual covers:
You need to set an appointment.
I don't know you.
We are not buying anything today.
We need to shop around.
It's too much money.
We don't want to put any money down.
Not doing anything till next year.

Some of the closes The Grant Cardone Rebuttal Manual teaches:
The Handshake Close
The Congratulations Close
Selection Alternative Close
Payment Breakdown Close
The Justifier Close
Price Guarantee Close

ABOUT THE AUTHOR

G. Cardone is an international sales expert, sales trainer, motivational speaker and New York Times best-selling author. He is known for customizing sales programs for organizations of all sizes and has positively affected hundreds of thousands of people and organizations worldwide. Fortune 500 companies, entrepreneurs, non-profit organizations, and individuals use his techniques and systems to increase their effectiveness and value in the marketplace.

Cardone is the star of National Geographic Channel's show, Turnaround King and is a regular contributor on Fox News, CNBC, MSNBC, and CNN. He has been speaking to audiences around the world for over twenty years on sales, success, finance, real estate, and motivation. His dynamic energy and his humorous and fast-paced delivery keep audiences entertained, intrigued, and involved.

Cardone is CEO of two training and consulting companies and owns a real estate investment and development firm worth more than $100 million in real estate holdings.

Objections in Prospecting (Door or Phone)

Objection **Not interested.**
Listen   Do not interrupt, listen to duplicate

Acknowledge   I hear that you are not interested and I
                understand. I take full responsibility for that.

Isolate   Other than you not being interested, is there any
                other reason that would keep you from giving me a
                couple minutes of your time?

Validate   The fact that you don't think your interested wouldn't
Discount   keep you from at least giving me shot would it?
                No –> transition into Qualifying
                Yes –> transition to Probe

Probe   Why is that?
                When you say that what do you mean?

Tie Down   Assuming that I could show you how I can improve
                your current situation, could you make 3 minutes for
                me now?

Justify & Close   If yes move to elevator pitch/Value Proposition

7

Objections in Prospecting (Door or Phone)

Objection	**You need to set an appointment.**
Listen	Do not interrupt, listen to duplicate
Acknowledge	I hear that you would like me to set an appointment and I understand.
Isolate	Other than me setting an appointment, is there any reason that you wouldn't give me a few minutes of your time?
Valid/Disc	Not having an appointment wouldn't keep you from looking at something that could dramatically improve your situation would it? No –> transition into Qualifying Yes -> transition to Probe
Probe	Why is that? When you say that what do you mean?
Tie Down	Assuming that I could show you how I can improve your current situation, could you make 3 minutes for me now?
Justify & Close	If yes move to elevator pitch/Value Proposition

Objections in Prospecting (Door or Phone)

Objection   **I don't have the time.**
Listen   Do not interrupt, listen to duplicate

Acknowledge   I hear that you don't have the time and I understand.

Isolate   Other than you not having the time, is there any reason that you wouldn't give me a few minutes so I could show you what my company can do for you?

Valid/Disc   Not having the time wouldn't keep you from looking at something that could dramatically improve your situation would it?
      No –> transition into Qualifying
      Yes -> transition to Probe

Probe   Why is that?
      When you say that what do you mean?

Tie Down   Assuming that I could show you how I can improve your current situation, could you make 3 minutes for me now?

Justify & Close   If yes move to elevator pitch/Value Proposition

Objections in Prospecting (Door or Phone)

Objection	**I don't know you.**
Listen	Do not interrupt, listen to duplicate
Acknowledge	I hear you. I understand that you don't know me. I accept full responsibility for that .
Isolate	Other than you not knowing me, is there any reason that you wouldn't give me a few minutes so I could show you what my company can do for you?
Valid/Disc	Look, not knowing me wouldn't keep you from looking at something that could dramatically improve your situation would it? No –> transition into Qualifying Yes -> transition to Probe
Probe	Why is that? When you say that what do you mean?
Tie Down	Assuming that I could show you how I can improve your current situation, could you make 3 minutes for me now?
Justify & Close	If yes move to elevator pitch/Value Proposition

Objections in Prospecting (Door or Phone)

Objection	**What are you doing here / Why are you here.**
Listen	Do not interrupt, listen to duplicate
Acknowledge	I understand that you would be wondering why I am here
Isolate	Other than you not knowing why I am here, is there any reason that you wouldn't give me a few minutes so I could show you what my company can do for you?
Valid/Disc	Look, not knowing me or why I am here wouldn't keep you from looking at something that could dramatically improve your situation would it? No –> transition into Qualifying Yes -> transition to Probe
Probe	Why is that? When you say that what do you mean?
Tie Down	Assuming that I could show you how I can improve your current situation, could you make 3 minutes for me now?
Justify & Close	If yes move to elevator pitch/Value Proposition

Objections in Prospecting (Door or Phone)

Objection   **Solicitors are not welcome here.**
Listen   Do not interrupt, listen to duplicate

Acknowledge   I hear you. I understand solicitors are not welcome here. I accept full responsibility for that .

Isolate   Other than solicitors not being allowed here, is there any reason that you wouldn't give me a few minutes so I could show you what my company can do for you?

Valid/Disc   Look, not knowing me or my company wouldn't keep you from looking at something that could dramatically improve your situation would it?
                 No –> transition into Qualifying
                 Yes -> transition to Probe

Probe   Why is that?
                 When you say that what do you mean?

Tie Down   Assuming that I could show you how I can improve your current situation, could you make 3 minutes for me now?

Justify & Close   If yes move to elevator pitch/Value Proposition

Objections in Prospecting (Door or Phone)

Objection   **Call my Assistant.**

Listen   Do not interrupt, listen to duplicate

Acknowledge   I hear you. I understand that you want me to call your assistant.

Isolate   Other than me calling your assistant is there any reason that you wouldn't give me a few minutes so I could show you what my company can do for you?

Valid/Disc   Look, not knowing me wouldn't keep you from looking at something that could dramatically improve your situation would it?
                    No –> transition into Qualifying
                    Yes -> transition to Probe

Probe   Why is that?
             When you say that what do you mean?

Tie Down   Assuming that I could show you how I can improve your current situation, could you make 3 minutes for me now?

Justify & Close   If yes move to elevator pitch/Value Proposition

Objections in Prospecting (Door or Phone)

Objection   **Send me some information.**

Listen   Do not interrupt, listen to duplicate

Acknowledge   I hear you. I understand that you would like me to send you some information, I would be happy to send it.

Isolate   Is receiving some information the only thing that is keeping you from giving me some time?

Valid/Disc   Look, not having the information first wouldn't keep you from looking at something that could dramatically improve your situation would it?
    No –> transition into Qualifying
    Yes -> transition to Probe

Probe   Why is that?
    When you say that what do you mean?

Tie Down   Assuming that I could show you how I can improve your current situation, could you make 3 minutes for me now?

Justify & Close   If yes move to elevator pitch/Value Proposition

14

Objections in Prospecting (Door or Phone)

Objection   **We are out of season.**

Listen   Do not interrupt, listen to duplicate

Acknowledge   I hear you. I understand that you are out of season. I accept full responsibility for that.

Isolate   Is the fact that you are out of season the only thing that is keeping you from giving me some time?

Valid/Disc   Being out of season wouldn't keep you from looking at something that could dramatically improve your situation would it?
                No –> transition into Qualifying
                Yes -> transition to Probe

Probe   Why is that?
           When you say that what do you mean?

Tie Down   Assuming that I could show you how I can improve your current situation, could you make 3 minutes for me now?

Justify & Close   If yes move to elevator pitch/Value Proposition

15

Objections in Prospecting (Door or Phone)

Objection   **Already working with someone.**

Listen   Do not interrupt, listen to duplicate

Acknowledge   I hear you. I understand that you are already working with someone. I accept responsibility for that.

Isolate   Is the fact the you are currently working with someone else the only thing keeping you from giving me some time today?

Valid/Disc   I understand, but would the fact that you are already working with someone keep you from looking at something that could dramatically improve your situation would it?
                No –> transition into Qualifying
                Yes -> transition to Probe

Probe   Why is that?
                When you say that what do you mean?

Tie Down   Assuming that I could show you how I can improve your current situation, could you make 3 minutes for me now?

Justify & Close   If yes move to elevator pitch/Value Proposition

Objections in Prospecting (Door or Phone)

Objection   **Call me another time, now is not good.**
Listen   Do not interrupt, listen to duplicate

Acknowledge   I hear you. I understand that you would like me to call you at another time.

Isolate   Is now not being a good time the only thing that is keeping you from giving me some time today?

Valid/Disc   You wouldn't let a few minutes of your time keep you from looking at something that could dramatically improve your situation would you?
                   No –> transition into Qualifying
                   Yes -> transition to Probe

Probe   Why is that?
                When you say that what do you mean?

Tie Down   Assuming that I could show you how I can improve your current situation, could you make 3 minutes for me now?

Justify & Close   If yes move to elevator pitch/Value Proposition

Objections in Prospecting (Door or Phone)

Objection   **Not a fan of your company.**

Listen   Do not interrupt, listen to duplicate

Acknowledge   I hear you. I understand that you are not a fan of our company. I accept full responsibility for that.

Isolate   Is you not being a fan of our company the only thing that is keeping you from giving me some time?

Valid/Disc   You wouldn't allow the fact that you are not a fan of our company to keep you from looking at something that could dramatically improve your situation would you?
        No –> transition into Qualifying
        Yes -> transition to Probe

Probe   Why is that?
       When you say that what do you mean?

Tie Down   Assuming that I could show you how I can improve your current situation, could you make 3 minutes for me now?

Justify & Close   If yes move to elevator pitch/Value Proposition

18

Objections in Prospecting (Door or Phone)

Objection   **I think you are a scam / heard you were a pyramid scheme.**

Listen   Do not interrupt, listen to duplicate

Acknowledge   I hear you. I understand that you heard that we were a scam. I accept full responsibility for that.

Isolate   Is the fact that you heard we are a scam the only thing that is keeping you from giving me some time?

Valid/Disc   You wouldn't allow the fact that you heard from someone that this is a scam to keep you from at least looking at something that could dramatically improve your situation would you?
          No –> transition into Qualifying
          Yes -> transition to Probe

Probe   Why is that?
          When you say that what do you mean?

Tie Down   Assuming that I could show you how I can improve your current situation, could you make 3 minutes for me now?

Justify & Close   If yes move to elevator pitch/Value Proposition

Objections in Greeting

Objection   **We are just looking.**

Listen   Do not interrupt, listen to duplicate

Acknowledge   I hear you. I understand that you are just looking.

Isolate   Is the fact that you are just looking the only thing that is that is keeping you from giving me some time?

Valid/Disc   You wouldn't allow the fact that you are just looking keep you from taking some time to look at something that could dramatically improve your situation would you?

       No –> transition into Qualifying
       Yes -> transition to Probe

Probe   Why is that?
       When you say that what do you mean?

Tie Down   Assuming that I could show you how I can improve your current situation, could you make 3 minutes for me now?

Justify & Close   If yes move to elevator pitch/Value Proposition

Objections in Greeting

Objection **We are just starting.**
Listen   Do not interrupt, listen to duplicate

Acknowledge   I hear you. I understand that you are just starting.

Isolate   Is the fact that you are just starting the only thing that is that is keeping you from giving me some time?

Valid/Disc   You wouldn't allow the fact that you are just starting from at least looking at something that could dramatically improve your situation would you?
                No –> transition into Qualifying
                Yes -> transition to Probe

Probe   Why is that?
           When you say that what do you mean?

Tie Down   Assuming that I could show you how I can improve your current situation, could you make 3 minutes for me now?

Justify & Close   If yes move to elevator pitch/Value Proposition

Objections in Greeting

Objection	**You are wasting your time.**
Listen	Do not interrupt, listen to duplicate
Acknowledge	I hear you. I understand that you think I am wasting my time.
Isolate	Is the fact that you think that I am wasting my time the only thing that is that is keeping you from giving me a shot?
Valid/Disc	You wouldn't allow the fact that you think that I am wasting my time keep you from at least looking at something that could dramatically improve your situation would you? No –> transition into Qualifying Yes -> transition to Probe
Probe	Why is that? When you say that what do you mean?
Tie Down	Assuming that I could show you how I can improve your current situation, could you make 3 minutes for me now?
Justify & Close	If yes move to elevator pitch/Value Proposition

Objections in Greeting

Objection   **I don't want to waste my time.**
Listen   Do not interrupt, listen to duplicate

Acknowledge   I hear you. I understand that you don't want to waste your time.

Isolate   Is the fact that you don't want to waste your time the only thing that is that is keeping you from giving me some time?

Valid/Disc   You wouldn't allow the fact that you don't want to waste your time to keep you from at least looking at something that could dramatically improve your situation would you?
                No –> transition into Qualifying
                Yes -> transition to Probe

Probe   Why is that?
                When you say that what do you mean?

Tie Down   Assuming that I could show you how I can improve your current situation, could you make 3 minutes for me now?

Justify & Close   If yes move to elevator pitch/Value Proposition

23

Objections in Greeting

Objection   **We are not buying anything today.**

Listen   Do not interrupt, listen to duplicate

Acknowledge   I hear you. I understand that you are not buying anything today.

Isolate   Is the fact that you are not buying anything today the only thing that is that is keeping you from giving me some time?

Valid/Disc   You wouldn't allow the fact that you are not buying anything today keep you from at least looking at something that could dramatically improve your situation would you?
                    No –> transition into Qualifying
                    Yes -> transition to Probe

Probe   Why is that?
                When you say that what do you mean?

Tie Down   Assuming that I could show you how I can improve your current situation, could you make 3 minutes for me now?

Justify & Close   If yes move to elevator pitch/Value Proposition

Objections in Greeting

Objection   **Leave me alone.**
Listen   Do not interrupt, listen to duplicate

Acknowledge   I hear you. I understand that you want me to leave you alone.

Isolate   Is the fact that you want me to leave you alone the only thing that is that is keeping you from giving me some time?

Valid/Disc   You wouldn't allow the fact that you want me to leave you alone to keep you from at least looking at something that could dramatically improve your situation would you?
No –> transition into Qualifying
Yes -> transition to Probe

Probe   Why is that?
When you say that what do you mean?

Tie Down   Assuming that I could show you how I can improve your current situation, could you make 3 minutes for me now?

Justify & Close   If yes move to elevator pitch/Value Proposition

25

Objections in Greeting

Objection   **We are just gathering information.**
Listen   Do not interrupt, listen to duplicate

Acknowledge   I hear you. I understand that you are just gathering information today.

Isolate   Is the fact that you are not buying anything today the only thing that is that is keeping you from giving me some time?

Valid/Disc   You wouldn't allow the fact that you are not buying anything today keep you from at least looking at something that could dramatically improve your situation would you?
                  No –> transition into Qualifying
                  Yes -> transition to Probe

Probe   Why is that?
               When you say that what do you mean?

Tie Down   Assuming that I could show you how I can improve your current situation, could you make 3 minutes for me now?

Justify & Close   If yes move to elevator pitch/Value Proposition

Objections in Greeting

Objection   **We don't know what we want yet.**
Listen   Do not interrupt, listen to duplicate

Acknowledge   I hear you. I understand that you don't know what you want yet.

Isolate   Is the fact that you don't know what you want yet the only thing that is that is keeping you from giving me some time?

Valid/Disc   You wouldn't allow the fact that you are not buying anything today keep you from at least looking at something that could dramatically improve your situation would you?
               No –> transition into Qualifying
               Yes -> transition to Probe

Probe   Why is that?
               When you say that what do you mean?

Tie Down   Assuming that I could show you how I can improve your current situation, could you make 3 minutes for me now?

Justify & Close   If yes move to elevator pitch/Value Proposition

Objections in Greeting

Objection	**How much is your product.**
Listen	Do not interrupt, listen to duplicate
Acknowledge	I hear you. I understand that you want to know how much our product is.
Isolate	Is the fact that you don't know how much the product costs the only thing that is that is keeping you from giving me some time?
Valid/Disc	You wouldn't allow the fact that you don't know how much the product costs from at least looking at something that could dramatically improve your situation would you? No –> transition into Qualifying Yes -> transition to Probe
Probe	Why is that? When you say that what do you mean?
Tie Down	Assuming that I could show you how I can improve your current situation, could you make 3 minutes for me now?
Justify & Close	If yes move to elevator pitch/Value Proposition

28

Objections in Qualifying

Objection	**We don't know what we want.**
Listen	Do not interrupt, listen to duplicate
Acknowledge	I hear you. I understand that you don't know what you want yet.
Isolate	Is the fact that you don't know what you want the only thing that is that is keeping you from learning more about what we do?
Valid/Disc	You wouldn't allow the fact that you don't know what you want from at least looking at something that could dramatically improve your situation would you?
	No –> transition into Qualifying
	Yes -> transition to Probe
Probe	Why is that?
	When you say that what do you mean?
Tie Down	Assuming that I could show you how I can improve your current situation, could you make 3 minutes for me now?
Justify & Close	If yes move into Fact Finding

Objections in Qualifying

Objection   **We are not buying anything today.**
Listen   Do not interrupt, listen to duplicate

Acknowledge   I hear you. I understand that you are not buying anything today.

Isolate   Is the fact that you are not buying anything today the only thing that is that is keeping you from giving me some time?

Valid/Disc   You wouldn't allow the fact that you are not buying anything today keep you from learning more about what we do, would you?
                No –> transition into Qualifying
                Yes -> transition to Probe

Probe   Why is that?
                When you say that what do you mean?

Tie Down   Assuming that I could show you how I can improve your current situation, could you make 3 minutes for me now?

Justify & Close   If yes move into Fact Finding

Objections in Qualifying

Objection	**I don't have time for this.**
Listen	Do not interrupt, listen to duplicate
Acknowledge	I hear you. I understand that you don't have time for this.
Isolate	Is the fact that you don't have time for this the only thing that is that is keeping you from giving me some time?
Valid/Disc	You wouldn't allow the fact that you don't have time for this keep you from learning more about how we an help improve your situation would you? No –> transition into Qualifying Yes -> transition to Probe
Probe	Why is that? When you say that what do you mean?
Tie Down	Assuming that I could show you how I can improve your current situation, could you make 3 minutes for me now?
Justify & Close	If yes move into Fact Finding

Objections in Qualifying

Objection   **What is your best price.**
Listen   Do not interrupt, listen to duplicate

Acknowledge   I hear you. I understand that you want our best price, I am happy to provide that to you.

Isolate   Is the fact that you want our best price the only thing that is that is keeping you from giving me some time?

Valid/Disc   You wouldn't allow the fact that you want the best price keep you from learning more about how we can help improve your situation would you?
     No –> transition into Qualifying
     Yes -> transition to Probe

Probe   Why is that?
When you say that what do you mean?

Tie Down   Assuming that I could show you how I can improve your current situation, could you make 3 minutes for me now?

Justify & Close   If yes move into Fact Finding

Objections in Qualifying

Objection   **I am not the decision maker.**

Listen   Do not interrupt, listen to duplicate

Acknowledge   I hear you. I understand that you are not the decision maker.

Isolate   Is the fact that you are not the decision maker the only thing that is that is keeping you from giving me some time?

Valid/Disc   You wouldn't allow the fact that you are not the decision maker keep you from learning more about how we can help improve your situation would you?
                No –> transition into Qualifying
                Yes -> transition to Probe

Probe   Why is that?
                When you say that what do you mean?

Tie Down   Assuming that I could show you how I can improve your current situation, could you make 3 minutes for me now?

Justify & Close   If yes move into Fact Finding

Objections in Qualifying

Objection	**Why do you need to know that?**
Listen	Do not interrupt, listen to duplicate
Acknowledge	I hear you. I understand that you want to know why we need to know that.
Isolate	Is the fact that you don't know why I am asking the only thing that is that is keeping you from giving me some more time and information?

Valid/Disc	You wouldn't allow the fact that you don't know why I am asking you these questions to keep you from learning more about how we can help improve your situation would you?
	    No –> transition into Qualifying
	    Yes -> transition to Probe

Probe	Why is that? When you say that what do you mean?
Tie Down	Assuming that I could show you how I can improve your current situation, could you make 3 minutes for me now?
Justify & Close	If yes move into Fact Finding

Objections in Presentation

Objection   **That is not important to us.**

Listen   Do not interrupt, listen to duplicate

Acknowledge   I hear you. I understand that you do not think that it is important to you.

Isolate   Is the fact that you do not think that it is important the only thing that is that is keeping you from learning more about how/why it is important?

Valid/Disc   You wouldn't allow the fact that you don't think it is important to keep you from learning more about how it could benefit and improve your situation would you?
     No –> transition into Qualifying
     Yes -> transition to Probe

Probe   Why is that?
When you say that what do you mean?

Tie Down   Assuming that I could show you how this can improve your current situation, would you be open to learning more about how it could benefit you?

Justify & Close   If yes move into/continue Presentation

Objections in Presentation

Objection   **What is your best price?**

Listen   Do not interrupt, listen to duplicate

Acknowledge   I hear you. I understand that you are looking for our best price.

Isolate   Is the fact that you want our best price the only thing that is that is keeping you from learning more about why what we do is important?

Valid/Disc   You wouldn't allow the fact that you want our best price keep you from learning more about how we can help improve your situation would you?
        No –> transition into Qualifying
        Yes -> transition to Probe

Probe   Why is that?
        When you say that what do you mean?

Tie Down   Assuming that I could show you how this can improve your current situation, would you be open to learning more about how it could benefit you?

Justify & Close   If yes move into Presentation

Objections in Presentation

Objection   **Not listening to you (this IS an objection).**

Listen   Do not interrupt, listen to duplicate

Acknowledge   I hear you. I understand that are not listening to me

Isolate   Is the fact that you do not think that it is important the only thing that is that is keeping you from learning more about how/why it is important?

Valid/Disc   You wouldn't allow the fact that you keep you from learning more about how we can help improve your situation would you?
        No –> transition into Qualifying
        Yes -> transition to Probe

Probe   Why is that?
    When you say that what do you mean?

Tie Down   Assuming that I could show you how this can improve your current situation, would you be open to learning more about how it could benefit you?

Justify & Close   If yes move into Presentation

Objections in Presentation

Objection   **Your competition has X.**
Listen   Do not interrupt, listen to duplicate

Acknowledge   I hear you. I understand that our competition has X.

Isolate   Is the fact that our competition has X the only thing that is that is keeping you from learning more about why what do is important?

Valid/Disc   You wouldn't allow the fact that our competition has X keep you from learning more about how we can help improve your situation would you?
                No –> transition into Qualifying
                Yes -> transition to Probe

Probe   Why is that?
                When you say that what do you mean?

Tie Down   Assuming that I could show you how this can improve your current situation, would you be open to learning more about how it could benefit you?

Justify & Close   If yes move into/continue Presentation

GC.

Objections in Presentation

Objection   **What are the terms going to be?**
Listen   Do not interrupt, listen to duplicate

Acknowledge   I hear you. I understand that you want to know the terms. I am happy to provide them.

Isolate   Is the fact that you want to know the terms are going to be the only thing that is that is keeping you from learning more about why what we do/have/offer is so valuable?

Valid/Disc   You wouldn't allow the fact that you want to know the terms keep you from learning more about how we can help improve your situation would you?
No –> transition into Qualifying
Yes -> transition to Probe

Probe   Why is that?
When you say that what do you mean?

Tie Down   Assuming that I could show you how this can improve your current situation, would you be open to learning more about how it could benefit you?

Justify & Close   If yes move into/continue Presentation

Objections in Presentation

Objection   **What is the warranty?**

Listen   Do not interrupt, listen to duplicate

Acknowledge   I hear you. I understand that you want to know warranty. I am happy to provide it.

Isolate   Is the fact that you want to know about the warranty the only thing that is that is keeping you from learning more about why what we do/have/offer is so valuable?

Valid/Disc   You wouldn't allow the fact that you want to know about the warranty keep you from learning more about how we can help improve your situation would you?
                    No –> transition into Qualifying
                    Yes -> transition to Probe

Probe   Why is that?
                When you say that what do you mean?

Tie Down   Assuming that I could show you how this can improve your current situation, would you be open to learning more about how it could benefit you?

Justify & Close   If yes move into Presentation

Objections in Presentation

Objection   **Is there a guarantee?**
Listen   Do not interrupt, listen to duplicate

Acknowledge   I hear you. I understand that you want to know if there is a guarantee.

Isolate   Is the fact that you want to know about a guarantee the only thing that is that is keeping you from learning more about why what we do/have/offer is so valuable?

Valid/Disc   You wouldn't allow the fact that you want to know if there is a guarantee keep you from learning more about how we can help improve your situation would you?
    No –> transition into Qualifying
    Yes -> transition to Probe

Probe   Why is that?
    When you say that what do you mean?

Tie Down   Assuming that I could show you how this can improve your current situation, would you be open to learning more about how it could benefit you?

Justify & Close   If yes move into Presentation

41

Objections in Presentation

Objection   **What service do you provide?**
Listen   Do not interrupt, listen to duplicate

Acknowledge   I hear you. I understand that you want to know about the service.

Isolate   Is the fact that you want to know about the service the only thing that is that is keeping you from learning more about why what we do/have/offer is so valuable?

Valid/Disc   You wouldn't allow the fact that you want to know about the service keep you from learning more about how we can help improve your situation would you?
                         No –> transition into Qualifying
                         Yes -> transition to Probe

Probe   Why is that?
                        When you say that what do you mean?

Tie Down   Assuming that I could show you how this can improve your current situation, would you be open to learning more about how it could benefit you?

Justify & Close   If yes move into Presentation

Objections in Presentation

Objection	How does this compare to X.
Listen	Do not interrupt, listen to duplicate
Acknowledge	I hear you. I understand that you want to know how this compares to X .
Isolate	Is the fact that you want to know how this compares to X the only thing that is that is keeping you from learning more about why what we do/have/offer is so valuable?
Valid/Disc	You wouldn't allow the fact that you want to know how this compares to X keep you from learning more about how we can help improve your situation would you?
	No –> transition into Qualifying
	Yes -> transition to Probe
Probe	Why is that?
	When you say that what do you mean?
Tie Down	Assuming that I could show you how this can improve your current situation, would you be open to learning more about how it could benefit you?
Justify & Close	If yes move into Presentation

Objections to Proposal

Objection   **I want your best price.**
Listen   Do not interrupt, listen to duplicate

Acknowledge   I hear you. I understand that you want our best price.

Isolate   Is getting our best price the only concern that you
                     have? Is there anything else that would keep you
                     from moving forward?

Valid/Disc   You wouldn't allow the fact that you want our best
                     price keep you from seeing a proposal with some
                     different options would you?
                            No –> transition into Qualifying
                            Yes -> transition to Probe

Probe   Why is that?
                     When you say that what do you mean?

Tie Down   Assuming that I could show you our best price and
                     how this decision makes sense, when is the soonest
                     that we could get started?

Justify & Close   If Yes move into Close

                     If No, there is another objection that you have yet
                     to handle

Objections to Proposal

Objection	**Not ready to make a decision.**
Listen	Do not interrupt, listen to duplicate
Acknowledge	I hear you. I understand that you are not ready to make a decision. I accept full responsibility for that.
Isolate	Is the fact that you are not ready to make a decision the only concern that you have? Is there anything else that would keep you from moving forward?
Valid/Disc	You wouldn't allow the fact that you are not ready to make a decision keep you from at least seeing a proposal with some different options would you? No –> transition into Qualifying Yes -> transition to Probe
Probe	Why is that? When you say that what do you mean?
Tie Down	Assuming that I could satisfy all of your concerns and show you different options would you consider looking at a proposal even if you are not ready?
Justify & Close	If Yes move into Proposal
	If No, there is another objection that you have yet to handle

Objections to Proposal

Objection	**We need to shop around.**
Listen	Do not interrupt, listen to duplicate
Acknowledge	I hear you. I understand that you want to shop around.
Isolate	Is shopping around the only concern that you have? Is there anything else that would keep you from moving forward?
Valid/Disc	You wouldn't allow the fact that you want to shop around keep you from at least seeing a proposal with some different options would you? No –> transition into Qualifying Yes -> transition to Probe
Probe	Why is that? When you say that what do you mean?
Tie Down	Assuming that I could show you a proposal with our best price along with some different options, would you consider looking at a proposal today?
Justify & Close	If Yes move into Proposal
	If No, there is another objection that you have yet to handle

Objections to Proposal

Objection	**We need to get three quotes.**
Listen	Do not interrupt, listen to duplicate
Acknowledge	I hear you. I understand that you need to get 3 quotes.
Isolate	Is getting multiple quotes the only concern that you have? Is there anything else that would keep you from moving forward?
Valid/Disc	You wouldn't allow the fact that you need to get 3 quotes keep you from at least seeing a proposal from me with some different options would you? No –> transition into Qualifying Yes -> transition to Probe
Probe	Why is that? When you say that what do you mean?
Tie Down	Assuming that I could show you a proposal with our best price along with some different options, would you consider looking at a proposal today?
Justify & Close	If Yes move into Proposal
	If No, there is another objection that you have yet to handle

Objections to Proposal

Objection   **We don't sign contracts.**

Listen   Do not interrupt, listen to duplicate

Acknowledge   I hear you. I understand that you don't sign contracts.

Isolate   Is the contract the only concern that you have? Is there anything else that would keep you from moving forward?

Valid/Disc   You wouldn't allow the fact that you don't sign contracts keep you from at least seeing a proposal with some different options would you?
        No –> transition into Qualifying
        Yes -> transition to Probe

Probe   Why is that? When you say that what do you mean?

Tie Down   Assuming that I could show you a proposal with our best price along with some different options, would you consider looking at a proposal today?

Justify & Close   If Yes move into Proposal

    If No, there is another objection that you have yet to handle

Objections to Proposal

Objection	**We want a free trial**
Listen	Do not interrupt, listen to duplicate
Acknowledge	I hear you. I understand that you want a free trial.
Isolate	Is getting a free trial the only concern that you have? Is there anything else that would keep you from moving forward?
Valid/Disc	You wouldn't allow the fact that you want a free trial keep you from at least seeing a proposal with some different options would you?
	No –> transition into Qualifying
	Yes -> transition to Probe
Probe	Why is that? When you say that what do you mean?
Tie Down	Assuming that I could show you a proposal with our best price along with some different options, would you consider looking at a proposal today?
Justify & Close	If Yes move into Proposal
	If No, there is another objection that you have yet to handle

Objections to Proposal

Objection   **I want the contract price on a M2M agreement.**

Listen   Do not interrupt, listen to duplicate

Acknowledge   I hear you. I understand that you want the contract price on a M2M agreement.

Isolate   Is wanting the contract price on a month-to-month agreement the only concern that you have? Is there anything else that would keep you from moving forward?

Valid/Disc   You wouldn't allow the fact that you want the contract pricing on a month-to-month agreement keep you from at least seeing a proposal with some different options would you?
                No –> transition into Qualifying
                Yes -> transition to Probe

Probe   Why is that?
             When you say that what do you mean?

Tie Down   Assuming that I could show you a proposal with our best price along with some different options, would you consider looking at a proposal today?

Justify & Close   If Yes move into Proposal

If No, there is another objection that you have yet to handle

Objections to Proposal

Objection   **We don't pay setup/upfront fees.**
Listen   Do not interrupt, listen to duplicate

Acknowledge   I hear you. I understand that you don't pay setup fees.

Isolate   Is not paying a setup fee the only concern that you
                      have? Is there anything else that would keep you
                      from moving forward?

Valid/Disc   You wouldn't allow the fact that you don't pay setup
                      fees keep you from at least seeing a proposal with
                      some different options would you?
                                No –> transition into Qualifying
                                Yes -> transition to Probe

Probe   Why is that?
                      When you say that what do you mean?

Tie Down   Assuming that I could show you a proposal with our
                      best price along with some different options, would
                      you consider looking at a proposal today?

Justify & Close   If Yes move into Proposal

                      If No, there is another objection that you have yet
                      to handle

Objections to Proposal

Objection   **We have a really low price from your competitor.**
Listen   Do not interrupt, listen to duplicate

Acknowledge   I hear you. I understand that you have a low price
                from our competitor.

Isolate   Is you having a low price from our competitor the
                only concern that you have? Is there anything else
                that would keep you from moving forward?

Valid/Disc   You wouldn't allow the fact that you have a low price
                from one of our competitors keep you from at least
                seeing a proposal with some different options
                would you?
                    No –> transition into Qualifying
                    Yes -> transition to Probe

Probe   Why is that?
                When you say that what do you mean?

Tie Down   Assuming that I could show you a proposal with our
                best price along with some different options, would
                you consider looking at a proposal today?

Justify & Close   If Yes move into Proposal

                If No, there is another objection that you have yet
                to handle

Objections to Proposal

Objection   **We don't want to put any money down**

Listen   Do not interrupt, listen to duplicate

Acknowledge   I hear you. I understand that you want don't want to put any money down.

Isolate   Is not putting any money down the only concern that you have? Is there anything else that would keep you from moving forward?

Valid/Disc   You wouldn't allow the fact that you don't want to put any money down keep you from at least seeing a proposal with some different options would you?
     No –> transition into Qualifying
     Yes -> transition to Probe

Probe   Why is that?
     When you say that what do you mean?

Tie Down   Assuming that I could show you a proposal with our best price along with some different options, would you consider looking at a proposal today?

Justify & Close   If Yes move into Proposal

     If No, there is another objection that you have yet to handle

Objections to Proposal

Objection   **We can secure our own financing**

Listen   Do not interrupt, listen to duplicate

Acknowledge   I hear you. I understand that you have your own financing.

Isolate   Is you having your own financing the only concern that you have? Is there anything else that would keep you from moving forward?

Valid/Disc   You wouldn't allow the fact that you have your own financing keep you from at least seeing a proposal with some different options would you?
         No –> transition into Qualifying
         Yes -> transition to Probe

Probe   Why is that?
         When you say that what do you mean?

Tie Down   Assuming that I could show you a proposal with our best price along with some different options, would you consider looking at a proposal today?

Justify & Close   If Yes move into Proposal

         If No, there is another objection that you have yet to handle

Objections to Proposal

Objection	**We are under contract with someone else.**
Listen	Do not interrupt, listen to duplicate
Acknowledge	I hear you. I understand that are under contract with someone else.
Isolate	Is being under contract with someone else the only concern that you have? Is there anything else that would keep you from moving forward?
Valid/Disc	You wouldn't allow the fact that you are under contract with someone else keep you from at least seeing a proposal with some different options would you?
	No –> transition into Qualifying
	Yes -> transition to Probe
Probe	Why is that?
	When you say that what do you mean?
Tie Down	Assuming that I could show you a proposal with our best price along with some different options, would you consider looking at a proposal today?
Justify & Close	If Yes move into Proposal
	If No, there is another objection that you have yet to handle

Objections to Proposal

Objection   **We don't have the budget this year.**
Listen   Do not interrupt, listen to duplicate

Acknowledge   I hear you. I understand that you don't have the budget this year.

Isolate   Is you not having the budget available this year the only concern that you have? Is there anything else that would keep you from moving forward?

Valid/Disc   You wouldn't allow the fact that you don't have any budget this year keep you from at least seeing a proposal with some different options would you?
    No –> transition into Qualifying
    Yes -> transition to Probe

Probe   Why is that?
    When you say that what do you mean?

Tie Down   Assuming that I could show you a proposal with our best price along with some different options, would you consider looking at a proposal today?

Justify & Close   If Yes move into Proposal

    If No, there is another objection that you have yet to handle

Objections to Proposal

Objection   **We want to wait for our tax refund.**
Listen   Do not interrupt, listen to duplicate

Acknowledge   I hear you. I understand that you want to wait for your tax refund.

Isolate   Is waiting for your tax refund the only concern that you have? Is there anything else that would keep you from moving forward?

Valid/Disc   You wouldn't allow the fact that you are waiting for your tax return keep you from at least seeing a proposal with some different options would you?
               No –> transition into Qualifying
               Yes -> transition to Probe

Probe   Why is that?
             When you say that what do you mean?

Tie Down   Assuming that I could show you a proposal with our best price along with some different options, would you consider looking at a proposal today?

Justify & Close   If Yes move into Proposal

              If No, there is another objection that you have yet to handle

Objections to Proposal

Objection   **We want to pay invoice.**
Listen   Do not interrupt, listen to duplicate

Acknowledge   I hear you. I understand that you want to pay invoice.

Isolate   Is paying invoice the only concern that you have? Is there anything else that would keep you from moving forward?

Valid/Disc   You wouldn't allow the fact that you want to pay invoice keep you from at least seeing a proposal with some different options would you?
                 No –> transition into Qualifying
                 Yes -> transition to Probe

Probe   Why is that?
               When you say that what do you mean?

Tie Down   Assuming that I could show you a proposal with our best price along with some different options, would you consider looking at a proposal today?

Justify & Close   If Yes move into Proposal

               If No, there is another objection that you have yet to handle

Objections to Close

Objection	**It's too much money.**
Listen	Do not interrupt, listen to duplicate

Acknowledge I hear you. I understand that you think it is too much money. I accept full responsibility for that.

Isolate Is the money the only concern that you have? Is there anything else that would keep you from moving forward?

Valid/Disc The fact that you think its too much money wouldn't keep you from owning this would you?
      No –> transition into Close
      Yes -> transition to Probe

Probe Why is that?
When you say that what do you mean?

Tie Down Assuming that I could make sense of the money for you could we finalize everything today?

Justify & Close If Yes move into Close with any Money closes necessary

If No, there is another objection that you have yet to handle

Objections to Close

Objection	**The cost is ridiculous, no way we would spend that much.**
Listen	Do not interrupt, listen to duplicate
Acknowledge	I hear you. I understand that you think the cost is ridiculous and that you would never spend that much. I accept full responsibility for that
Isolate	Is you thinking that the cost is ridiculous your only concern that you have? Is there anything else that would keep you from moving forward?
Valid/Disc	The fact that you think the cost is ridiculous wouldn't keep you from owning this would you? No –> transition into Close Yes -> transition to Probe
Probe	Why is that? When you say that what do you mean?
Tie Down	Assuming that I could make sense of the money and why our product is value priced could we finalize everything today?
Justify & Close	If Yes move into Close with any Money closes If No, there is another objection that you have yet to handle

Objections to Close

Objection   **It's more than our budget.**
Listen   Do not interrupt, listen to duplicate

Acknowledge   I hear you. I understand that it is more than
               your budget. I accept full responsibility for that.

Isolate   Is the budget the only concern that you have?
               Is there anything else that would keep you from
               moving forward?

Valid/Disc   The fact that it's more than you had budgeted for
               wouldn't keep you from owning this would you?
                    No –> transition into Close
                    Yes -> transition to Probe

Probe   Why is that?
               When you say that what do you mean?

Tie Down   Assuming that I could make sense of the money
               and how this fits in your budget could we finalize
               everything today?

Justify & Close   If Yes move into Close with any Budget closes

               If No, there is another objection that you have yet
               to handle

Objections to Close

Objection	**The payments are too high.**
Listen	Do not interrupt, listen to duplicate
Acknowledge	I hear you. I understand that you think the payments are too high.
Isolate	Are the payments the only concern that you have? Is there anything else that would keep you from moving forward?
Valid/Disc	The fact that it's more than you had budgeted for wouldn't keep you from owning this would you? No –> transition into Close Yes -> transition to Probe
Probe	Why is that? When you say that what do you mean?
Tie Down	Assuming that I could make sense of the money and how this fits in your budget could we finalize everything today?
Justify & Close	If Yes move into Close with any Budget closes
	If No, there is another objection that you have yet to handle

Objections to Close

Objection	**Call me when you can get where I want to be on the money.**
Listen	Do not interrupt, listen to duplicate
Acknowledge	I hear you. I understand that you want me to call you when I can get where you want to be on the money. I accept full responsibility for that.
Isolate	Is the money the only concern that you have? Is there anything else that would keep you from moving forward?
Valid/Disc	The fact that it's more than you want to spend wouldn't keep you from owning this would you? No –> transition into Close Yes -> transition to Probe
Probe	Why is that? When you say that what do you mean?
Tie Down	Assuming that I could make sense of the money and how this fits in your budget could we finalize everything today?
Justify & Close	If Yes move into Close with any Money/Budget closes
	If No, there is another objection that you have yet to handle

Objections to Close

Objection	**Send this all over to me in an email so I can review it.**
Listen	Do not interrupt, listen to duplicate
Acknowledge	I hear you. I understand that you want me to email you everything to review. I would be happy to do that.
Isolate	Is you reviewing the information the only concern that you have? Is there anything else that would keep you from moving forward?
Valid/Disc	The fact that you want to think about this wouldn't keep you from owning would it? No –> transition into Close Yes -> transition to Probe
Probe	Why is that? When you say that what do you mean?
Tie Down	Assuming that I could make sense of the money and how this fits in your budget could we finalize everything today?
Justify & Close	If Yes move into Close with any Money/Budget closes
	If No, there is another objection that you have yet to handle

Objections to Close

Objection   **I want your bottom line, best price, you have one shot.**
Listen   Do not interrupt, listen to duplicate

Acknowledge   I hear you. I understand that you want my absolute best price, I would be happy to get that for you.

Isolate   Is getting the best price the only concern that you have? Is there anything else that would keep you from moving forward?

Valid/Disc   The money wouldn't keep you from owning this would it?
                No –> transition into Close
                Yes –> transition to Probe

Probe   Why is that?
                When you say that what do you mean?

Tie Down   Assuming that I could make sense of the money and how this fits in your budget could we finalize everything today?

Justify & Close   If Yes move into Close with any Money/Budget closes

                If No, there is another objection that you have yet to handle

Objections to Close

Objection **We are not ready yet.**
Listen Do not interrupt, listen to duplicate

Acknowledge I hear you. I understand that you are not ready yet. I accept full responsibility for that.

Isolate Is you not being ready the only concern that you have? Is there anything else that would keep you from moving forward?

Valid/Disc The fact that it's more than you want to spend wouldn't keep you from owning this would you?
No --> transition into Close
Yes -> transition to Probe

Probe Why is that?
When you say that what do you mean?

Tie Down Assuming that I could make sense of the decision could we finalize everything today?

Justify & Close If Yes move into Close with any Stall closes

If No, there is another objection that you have yet to handle

Objections to Close

Objection	**I can get it cheaper elsewhere.**
Listen	Do not interrupt, listen to duplicate
Acknowledge	I hear you. I understand that you think you can get it cheaper elsewhere. I accept full responsibility for that.
Isolate	Is you being able to get it cheaper elsewhere the only concern that you have? Is there anything else that would keep you from moving forward?
Valid/Disc	The fact that you think you can get it cheaper wouldn't keep you from owning this would you? No –> transition into Close Yes –> transition to Probe
Probe	Why is that? When you say that what do you mean?
Tie Down	Assuming that I could make sense of the money and your how this fits in your budget could we finalize everything today?
Justify & Close	If Yes move into Close with any Money closes If No, there is another objection that you have yet to handle

Objections to Close

Objection	**We don't sign contracts.**
Listen	Do not interrupt, listen to duplicate

Acknowledge   I hear you. I understand that you don't sign contracts. I accept full responsibility for that.

Isolate   Is the fact that you don't sign contracts the only concern that you have? Is there anything else that would keep you from moving forward?

Valid/Disc   The fact that you don't sign contracts wouldn't keep you from owning this would you?
      No –> transition into Close
      Yes -> transition to Probe

Probe   Why is that?
When you say that what do you mean?

Tie Down   Assuming that I could make sense of the decision could we finalize everything today?

Justify & Close   If Yes move into Close with any Stall/Money/Budget closes

If No, there is another objection that you have yet to handle

Objections to Close

Objection   **I need to talk to our Board/Other Influencers.**
Listen   Do not interrupt, listen to duplicate

Acknowledge   I hear you. I understand that you want to talk about this with a few other people. I accept full responsibility for that.

Isolate   Is you talking to a few other people in your company the only concern that you have? Is there anything else that would keep you from moving forward?

Valid/Disc   The fact that you think its too much money wouldn't keep you from owning this would you?
No –> transition into Close
Yes -> transition to Probe

Probe   Why is that?
When you say that what do you mean?

Tie Down   Assuming that I could make sense of the decision for you could we finalize everything today?

Justify & Close   If Yes move into Close with any Stall/Money closes necessary

If No, there is another objection that you have yet to handle

Objections in Follow-up

Objection   **Not doing anything until next year.**

Listen   Do not interrupt, listen to duplicate

Acknowledge   I hear you. I understand that you are not going to do anything until next year. I accept full responsibility for that.

Isolate   Is waiting until next year the only concern that you have? Is there anything else that would keep you from moving forward?

Valid/Disc   The fact that you think its too much money wouldn't keep you from owning this would you?
     No –> transition into Close
     Yes -> transition to Probe

Probe   Why is that?
     When you say that what do you mean?

Tie Down   Assuming that I could make sense of the decision for you could we finalize everything today?

Justify & Close   If Yes move into Close with any Money closes necessary

     If No, there is another objection that you have yet to handle

Objections in Follow-up

Objection   **We are going with someone else.**
Listen   Do not interrupt, listen to duplicate

Acknowledge   I hear you. I understand that you are going with someone else. I accept full responsibility for that.

Isolate   Is you going with someone else the only thing keeping you from giving me time? Is there anything else that would keep you from moving forward?

Valid/Disc   The fact that you are going with someone else wouldn't keep you giving us one more shot at the deal would it?
                    No –> transition into Close
                    Yes -> transition to Probe

Probe   Why is that?
                When you say that what do you mean?

Tie Down   Assuming that I could make sense of the decision for you could we finalize everything today?

Justify & Close   If Yes move into Close with any Money closes necessary

                If No, there is another objection that you have yet to handle

71

Objections in Follow-up

Objection   **Decided not to do anything right now.**
Listen   Do not interrupt, listen to duplicate

Acknowledge   I hear you. I understand that you are not going to do
              anything right now. I accept full responsibility
              for that.

Isolate   Is waiting the only concern that you have?
              Is there anything else that would keep you from
              moving forward?

Valid/Disc   The fact that you think its too much money wouldn't
              keep you from owning this would you?
                  No –> transition into Close
                  Yes -> transition to Probe

Probe   Why is that?
              When you say that what do you mean?

Tie Down   Assuming that I could make sense of the decision for
              you could we finalize everything today?

Justify & Close   If Yes move into Close with any Money closes
              necessary

              If No, there is another objection that you have yet
              to handle

Objections in Follow-up

Objection   **No time to discuss right now.**
Listen   Do not interrupt, listen to duplicate

Acknowledge   I hear you. I understand that you don't have the time to discuss this. I accept full responsibility for that.

Isolate   Is not having the time to speak the only concern that you have? Is there anything else that would keep you from moving forward?

Valid/Disc   The fact that you don't have the time right now wouldn't keep you from looking at something that could dramatically improve your situation would it?
                No –> transition into Close
                Yes -> transition to Probe

Probe   Why is that?
            When you say that what do you mean?

Tie Down   Assuming that I could make sense of the decision for you could we finalize everything today?

Justify & Close   If Yes move into Close with any Money closes necessary

                If No, there is another objection that you have yet to handle

Objections in Follow-up

Objection   **Next time you are in the area, just call me.**
Listen   Do not interrupt, listen to duplicate

Acknowledge   I hear you. I understand that you want me to call you next time I am in the area. I accept full responsibility for that.

Isolate   Is me being in the area the only concern that you have? Is there anything else that would keep you from moving forward?

Valid/Disc   The fact you want me to come by next time I am in town wouldn't keep you from making a decision that could improve your situation would it?
                   No –> transition into Close
                   Yes -> transition to Probe

Probe   Why is that?
                   When you say that what do you mean?

Tie Down   Assuming that I could make sense of the decision for you could we finalize everything today?

Justify & Close   If Yes move into Close with any Money closes necessary

                   If No, there is another objection that you have yet to handle

Objections in Follow-up

Objection   **We are still shopping.**
Listen   Do not interrupt, listen to duplicate

Acknowledge   I hear you. I understand that you are still shopping. I accept full responsibility for that.

Isolate   Is wanting to shop the only concern that you have? Is there anything else that would keep you from moving forward?

Valid/Disc   The fact that want to shop around some more wouldn't keep you from owning would it?
                 No –> transition into Close
                 Yes -> transition to Probe

Probe   Why is that?
                 When you say that what do you mean?

Tie Down   Assuming that I could make sense of the decision for you could we finalize everything today?

Justify & Close   If Yes move into Close with any Money closes necessary

                 If No, there is another objection that you have yet to handle

Basic | Closes

Three Yeses and Close

"Did I answer all your questions? Were we easy to get to? Am I the type of person you'd feel comfortable, you know, having service you? Great. Then I need your okay here, here and here."

Referral Close

"Hey, before we get involved with the figures, who do you know that may be in the market for a similar purchase that you're making today?"

"Hey before we get involved with the figures, okay, before we you know actually customize your proposition. Who do you know that would be in the market for a similar product or service that you're considering today? Get a name, get a number; get a name, a phone number, and email address before you present figures to this customer."

The Handshake Close

"Hey look, you know John, it serves your needs. You know you can afford it. You know you're going to do it sooner or later. It's only a matter of time. Let's get this done right now."

Basic | Closes

The Ben Franklin Close

"You know I understand how hard it is to make a decision and it is said that Ben Franklin one of our founding fathers when faced with a big decision would actually sit down with a legal pad and write down the pluses and the minuses, accumulate all that information on a piece of paper so he could get a true accurate evaluation of what the right thing to do was. Pull out a sheet of paper now, so let me ask you John, what are the positives of this purchase? And list each positive. Now tell me this, what are the negatives? Once you have that list, use the advantages to outweigh the other and close the deal. I would say this sir, if you have more minuses than pluses don't do it and if you have more pluses than minuses, I would encourage you to go ahead and make the investment."

Basic | Closes

The Second Party Assist Close

"Hey John, if this figure, considering what you know about the product, and knowing your brother as you know your brother, what advice would you give him about the purchase of this product and the fairness of the figures."

Do It For Me Close

"Sir, if you can't do it for you, and you can't do it for your wife, let me suggest you do it for me. I need your OK here and here."

The Payoff Close

"So you agree to purchase now, assuming we can pay off the balance owed on your present lease or mortgage using the company's rebates and discounts, our rebates and discounts, or by getting the lender, I'm writing this all out, to carry the difference. John's funds, your funds, sir, will now be used to reduce the amount financed on the new purchase. I need your initials here and here."

Basic | Closes

The Eleventh Inning Close

"Hey what figures and what terms would be necessary for you to say yes to this purchase right now?"

The Scarcity Close

"As you are aware, there's a limited availability of this specific product, the one you want. A huge demand in the marketplace, and I want to be certain John, that I'm able to get you what you want. So look, I need to get this paperwork done, which means I need your approval here, here, and here, and I also need to know the delivery date that I can install, okay. Let's do this now."

The Puppy Dog Close

"Hey let me suggest that you go ahead and take it home tonight. We go ahead and get it installed. And when you wake up tomorrow, you decide whether it's the right thing for you to have done or not. If you decide it's not, we come back and pick it up. Or you can bring it back. And no problems. At least you will have had the experience of having it in your home."

Basic | Closes

Feel, Felt, Found, Close

"Hey I appreciate the way you feel. I have felt exactly the same way until I found out that I don't have another one coming in. The price will not get lower. And the bottom line is you need it, and you need it now man. Let's go ahead and do this. I need your full legal name right here by owner."

Second Baseman Close

"Will you be helping with the price, the down payment, the monthly payment, the paperwork, or John did you want to help with all three?"

"Man I'm not doing anything."

Good. Then if I can get this done without you being involved, would you suggest that he do it or not do it? Or B answer, he could say what?

"Hey I'll help with everything Grant. Whatever he needs help with I'll help him. That's my grandson right there."

Great. Then let's go over all the numbers so you know exactly what we're doing here and go into your presentation."

Basic | Closes

Second Baseman Close II

"So Sherry did you want me to work it out so it's affordable using just John's money that he or she has alone, or did you want me to plan you getting financially involved as well?"

The Delay Payment Close

"OK, John, so you will own now, assuming we can pay off your credit cards, save you make your current payment, and set it up to where you don't have any future payments for not just this month but next month, not until the following month. How does that work for you?"

The No-Cosigner Close

"So, John, assuming financing can be provided in your name with no other signatures necessary from anyone else, you agree to ownership now and agree to delivery at the figures disclosed. I need your approval right here."

Affordability | Objections
I don't think I can afford to do this

"Then how do you feel about what you're paying for your present vehicle? It's not what you want. It keeps going down in value. Let's do this."

"Do you think it's going to get any easier to afford it later? Look, when's the best time to do something nice for yourself? Let's do this now."

"When you say you're not sure you can afford it, do you mean the down payment, the monthly payments, the price, or the value of what I'm paying for yours? What exactly are you not sure of?"

"Look if I can't come up with some figures that make this affordable, easily affordable for you and your household, I would be the first to suggest you not purchase it, fair enough?"

"With the financing packages we have available today, I assure you that we will make this affordable and if we can't, I wouldn't ask you do business with us."

Basic | Closes

I don't think I can afford to do this

"Look if I can't show you a way to make this affordable, to make you dreams affordable and real, I wouldn't expect you to do business with us, let's go sit down and work it out."

"Look it's better to enjoy your life now then to say later that you didn't treat yourself well. You deserve to reward yourself. I need your full legal name here and here."

"That's what you heard. Look I know you don't have unlimited resources, neither do I, let's take a look at what you're working with, leave it up to me to make that work, is that agreeable?"

"Look, based on your new position, I'm not sure you can afford to continue driving what you own now. I need your okay here and here."

"I would say to you sir that you can't afford to be without a new car. Look, the cost of not having one is far greater than the small increase monthly investments, pass the pen."

Affordability | Objections
I don't think I can afford to do this

"Look, I'm surprised to hear you say that. You look the type of person that can easily afford this vehicle. Isn't that true? Now, I need you okay here, here, and here."

"Forgive me for being nosy, but what are you spending your money on? Look other than your home, what can be more important than investing in a quality automobile that projects the image you want and provides you and your household with a safety, comfort, and reliability of a new vehicle. Look, I need your approval here, here, and here. Let's get this done."

"Look, I sincerely believe that buying anything less than this is what you can't afford. You owe it to yourself, you owe it to your position, and look when you took that position, you took on a new image; let's do this."

"Look, it would be a shame to see you pass on this investment. It makes such a powerful statement about who you are. This product says you're a success and you deserve it. You want in your name, your company's name, or both?"

84

Affordability | Objections
I don't think I can afford to do this

"I don't think we can make sense of it, something like that. Look, this investment only looks like you can't afford it. I promise you, that we will work it out so that you can own what you want, own your dreams, and that they're affordable."

"Look, you're going to find the pleasure of owning this will far out way the small monthly outlay."

"Everyone that has ever bought from me, everyone that has ever made an investment in this product, has said exactly the same thing. Look taking into consideration the gas savings could save you 1200 dollars a year. The low interest rate is going to save you about 700 dollars a year. The warranty protection up to 3000 a year and the resale value and you'll find it's cheaper own new than own what you own now."

"Tell me would you rather own new or used if the payments were identical? You'd rather own new, then I need your approval here, here, and here, let's get this done."

Affordability | Objections
I don't think I can afford to do this

"Look, I understand your concern; it's natural that you would have that worry. Tell me, what present spending activity is getting in the way of you doing what you want to do? Let's work that out and you can have what you want."

"You've presented numbers and heard this. Look, if I was a betting man I'd be willing to bet that you're new purchase would be cheaper to operate and own than what you're doing right now. If so, which one would you rather do? Good. Now what I want you do is reduce the objection between you and your client to a difference in payments and close the deal."

"That's exactly why you should take ownership of this now. You guys have waited long enough to reward yourself with something new. Now who's going to be the first to say yes?"

"Look, very few people think they can afford to do anything until they look at the monthly outlay; allow me to make it a reality for you so you can do what you want. Let me show you how to make sense of this."

Affordability | Objections
I don't think I can afford to do this

"I can't even believe you said that, now knock off the negative talk. If you can't do it, no one can. I need you to sign here and here."

"Look, it's my responsibility to make it affordable. If I'm unable to do so, then we can always consider some alternatives, but let's stay with what you want and let me work it out. Fair enough?"

"What would you rather do? For a few more dollars a month which one would you rather do? Good, let's do it."

Sir, I make my living making things affordable. That means I'm in your employ. Allow me to work out the figures for you, if they don't fit, then you can either fire me or you can tell me what it is that we need to do to make you a happy owner. Fair enough?

Affordability | Objections
I don't think I can afford to do this

"Look, I assure you the vehicle itself is more than affordable. It's not the product you're buying the car, it's the extra conveniences that are affecting the price and the payments. Let me show what I mean. For instance, and you're going to go into payment breakdown now, take the GPS system, the full leather package, the 4-wheel drive, or whatever the case and show the difference in payments right there, this will make you deal."

"Hey, thanks for being so honest with me about your budget concerns. Let's see where it fits in your budget and if we can make it out, and what you are comfortable with otherwise I wouldn't expect you to buy. Now, how much is your rent? Insurance? Utilities? Alimony? Child support? Okay, whatever go through that list, you're going to find an extra cushion or the customer is going to justify going more into depth than they already are. They want to buy, just give them a justification."

Affordability | Objections
I don't think I can afford to do this

"Ask yourself then would you rather enjoy your life now or wait till later and enjoy it, or have somebody else enjoy your money later on when you're not here. Come on let's do this, you can do it."

"Look, with the value of your vehicle, the one you're getting rid of, the present interest rates and the promotion we have going on for the vehicle that you want, it will never, literally never be affordable, more affordable to you than right now. I need your approval here and here."

"Look, based on your present income and the expenses, if there was money left over, after which you could pay for the car and still pay for food and rent and utilities, medical, clothes, school, entertainment, and all the other things you need and save money would you define that as affordable? Great. Let's go through it."

"Look, is this some kind of fear that you experience every time you buy something? Now ask yourself, when's the last time you bought something you couldn't afford? Great. Let's do this."

89

Affordability | Objections
I don't think I can afford to do this

"Look, you guys go through this every time you do something nice for yourself? Come on really, when's the last the time you did something nice for yourself? It's time you did it again. Don't you agree? Let's do this."

"Look, very few people think they can afford to do anything until they look at the monthly outlay; allow me to make it a reality for you so you can do what you want. Let me show you how to make sense of this."

Prices too high again in the objection

"Hey, John we have reasons for it being priced that way, because of its limited production, high quality, and tremendous high resale value, this investment will prove to be the least expensive of all like investments that you have made in the past. Let's do this."

Difference Objections | Closes

The difference is too high

"It's not agreeable. Hey, I appreciate that. Let me ask you, what are you comparing this difference to?"

"Hey, it's only too much if you plan on taking care of the balance in full. And why would anybody want to do that?"

"Hey, when you say the difference is too high do you refer to that because of the price, the value we're paying for yours, or is it the payments that you're worried about? When you say too high what are you talking about?"

"Difference, I'm surprised you say that. I think we've been more than fair with you on both the value that we're selling our vehicle for and the figures that we're giving you for yours. Where do you feel like I'm being unfair with you?"

"And so one way to reduce the difference to get it lower is by you reducing it with cash or equity. Now how much would you like to reduce the difference by? Because I've done everything I can."

Difference Objections | Closes

The difference is too high

"Difference is too high and that reason that the difference is too high sir is when you bought your present vehicle and made a decision to keep your cash rather than reducing the balance, it causes this kind of situation now. So let's avoid doing the same thing this time by putting some more money down and reduce the difference. What do you think?"

"Hey that seems to be everyone's initial reaction. However, I assure you that the figures that I have here for you are excellent based on what you're buying and based on what you're getting. And the excellent choice you have made on this investment, so let's go ahead and take delivery on it so you can start enjoying it today."

"Difference is too high and I understand that this figure does not represent your net difference sir. Do you understand what I'm saying? This figure is your gross difference not your net difference. Allow me to share with you your true net difference. And what I want you to do right here now is reduce the difference by what resale value they're going to get from this product in the future."

Difference Objections | Closes

The difference is too high

"Look, all things can be adjusted. Let me ask you, do you have to sell your vehicle to buy the new one? 'Oh yeah I have to.' Good, then let's focus back on the trade and show the buyer why we're showing him that number for their vehicle and justify that. "

"So the enjoyment, the peace of mind, and the feelings that go along with owning this product will far outweigh the little bit of difference that you might not agree with. Let's get this done."

"Then allow me to work it out for you, John, OK? Look, there's a number of ways we could reduce the difference. Number one, remove some of the additions we've made to your new purchase. Number two, we could have your car looked at again and see if we can have someone pay a little extra. I don't think that's possible, but we can try. And number three, use some of your cash to reduce the difference, which is the best way to control a difference and lower your monthly investments. Number four, we could consider a combination of all four of those steps. Look, you're the boss. Tell me how you'd like to do it."

93

Difference Objections | Closes

The difference is too high

"Hey John, you need to know this, OK? My boss wanted me to present a number to you a great deal higher than what I'm showing you right here. But I worked with him to get that number down. Now let me ask you: What number were you thinking of?"

"Okay. I got it. Now let me answer. Are you in a position to sell your vehicle yourself? Because if you were willing to do that, you could probably reduce your difference by maybe $500 or $600, maybe $800. Would that be worth your time and energy and the worry that still goes into selling a car independently with people coming over to your house that you don't know? Look, encourage this buyer to say yes to selling. Then use the calculations shown in the other trade segments to close in on this difference."

"Sir, that's why we have alternatives for people that pay the difference over time. Look, allow us to tailor a payment plan that would make this difference affordable for you. Let's face it. The difference is based on what you want. Let's do this.

Difference Objections | Closes
The difference is too high

"Yes, sir. And the difference properly reflects the performance, the quality and the choice you've made in this investment. Now, is this going to be in your name or your company's name? Let's get this done."

"That's what they're telling you. And that's more of the reason for making a decision to do this today. Look, waiting has already cost you too much money. Putting it off will only make it worse. Do you understand? If you'd had done this a year ago, the difference would be this much lower. Let's go ahead and get this done."

"That's exactly why I would suggest, sir, you quit holding onto your vehicles so long before replacing them. Look, you're calling this the difference because of the length of time of ownership. Now, let's get this done before it gets any worse."

Difference Objections | Closes

The difference is too high

"Then sir, would you consider looking at a car like I suggested earlier that would have low miles, a full written warranty. Might save yourself $1,000, maybe $800, maybe only $500 but it would reduce the difference."

"Great, John, so would you work with me on the amount of the difference that you can live with?"

"I can understand that sir. And let me remind you it's my responsibility to work it out so that we come up with something you can live with. Suppose we could provide you with some additional value at a reduced cost to you. The difference would be the same, but I would increase what you are getting."

Down Payment | Closes

Too much money down

"Sir, when you say too much money down, does that mean the funds are not available? Or that you're just not comfortable with using that amount to reduce the balance?"

"Hey John, before you commit to that, before you commit to saying it's too much, allow me to share with you some of the benefits that you'd receive by putting that amount down. First of all it reduces your monthly payments. Number two, it's going to reduce the overall interest on the loan. Number three, it's going reduce the overall payments and allow you to be in a situation where you have equity and pay the vehicle off sooner. Let's do this."

"I understand how you feel. John, however, allow me to share the benefits with you from using that amount. Lower payments, less interest, shorter time, peace of mind. You don't need to worry about the payments every night. And you have constant equity from day one. Let's make sense of this and do it."

97

Down Payment | Closes
Too much money down

"No problem. Hey let's look at a situation where you would be using that amount down so you can compare what is recommended to whatever you decide. Is that fair enough? See what you want to do here is make your buyer responsible for the amount of down payment and monthly payment."

"John, I didn't say you had to put that much money down. What I'm saying is that's the amount requested by the bank. Now what portion of that amount are you in a position to use as equity and thereby reduce your monthly cost?"

"John, I'm surprised that you say that it's too much money down. You seem like the kind of individual that would want to put more down, provide yourself and your family with a lower monthly cost. Come on, let's do this."

"I agree. Since you don't like putting your cash into the purchase, would you consider a way to keep all your cash and be able to replace products at regular intervals with no money down?"

Down Payment | Closes
Too much money down

"Okay, besides the equity we're requesting, how do you feel about all of the other figures? Okay, assume I can work with you on the down payment and still keep all the other terms agreeable. Do you have any other reasons, any other reasons not to purchase now?"

"Yeah, I understand and it seems like it's a big amount until we examine what 1/3 down would do for you. You know, part of that amount is covering your taxes, your license which is controlled by the state. And the remainder is providing you with equity on the day you drive off. Look, would you prefer paying for the taxes over a period of time, financing and then paying interest on top of that? If not, let's make this work."

Down Payment | Closes

Too much money down

"Hey, I certainly understand if you're not in a position to put more down. But then that's not really your situation is it?"

"What do you mean Grant?"

"Well is the issue that you don't want to put the money down or you can't? What you want to do is find that out here."

"Look, I know it seems like that now but understand the money you invest now remains invested in this product, in this investment now allowing you to be in a much better position or place and negotiate the next time you want to move up. As well as provide you with lower payments and protect your down payment so that you know you have it in the future."

Down Payment | Closes

Too much money down

"Excellent sir. If you're not going to use that amount down I would strongly suggest that we consider then talking to our bank representative about an alternative way to get you into this purchase with less money down. Let me ask you, what are you thinking about as a down payment so I can bring him here."

"Certainly John, you were figuring somewhere close to that amount. What were you thinking?"

"It's a lot of money down. The down payment's too much. John, that's the amount sufficient to support you and me and put your family in a position where we can actually pay off your vehicle and still have enough money to qualify you for preferred rates. How close to this figure can you get?"

Down Payment | Closes

Too much money down

"Well how about this. How about we provide you with the money down? What do you mean by that? We're going to provide you with the down payment, get a second loan on that amount so that you're in a position to have equity on the first purchase now and pay off the second loan when you can."

"Okay great. So would you rather keep your cash or some portion of it and pay a little more on a monthly basis?"

"Yeah Grant, that's what I want to do."

"Good." Go into that negotiation with the buyer."

Down Payment | Closes

Too much money down

"Excellent sir. If you're not going to use that amount down I would strongly suggest that we consider then talking to our bank representative about an alternative way to get you into this purchase with less money down. Let me ask you, what are you thinking about as a down payment so I can bring him here."

"Certainly John, you were figuring somewhere close to that amount. What were you thinking?"

"It's a lot of money down. The down payment's too much. John, that's the amount sufficient to support you and me and put your family in a position where we can actually pay off your vehicle and still have enough money to qualify you for preferred rates. How close to this figure can you get?"

Money | Closes

"Hey, if the payments aren't agreeable, we wouldn't expect you to buy the product. I'm confident that our choice of lenders can provide you with alternatives that will make your monthly investments agreeable and affordable."

Payments to Figure Close

"Buyer says, hey, what are my payments going to be? Sir, until you and I come to an agreement on the price, the product, and the terms, you really don't need to concern yourself with payments because there won't be any. Look, I need your initial here, here, and here on what? Price and terms, not just the payments."

What are the rates?

"We use every lender in the state including every credit union. Who do you use? We have access to everyone and including the people you use now. Look, there's only a couple of people in town cheaper than your lender. Sign right here and I'll look at all our other options. Worst case is we go back to your present lender."

Money | Closes

Agreement Close 1

"I agree it's a lot of money. I need your okay here and here."

Agreement Close 2

"I agree it's a lot of money and expect that you knew that before you even got here. Before you even started looking at this you knew it was a lot of money. Now, I need your OK here and here."

Agreement Close 3

"I agree, and everyone that has ever bought this product said exactly the same thing. I need your approval here, here and here."

Money | Closes

The Be Grateful Close

"I agree with you, and be grateful that you can even consider investing this much money. You know, not everyone can do this. There's people on this planet starving and look at you, you're investing in your company. You're investing in new equipment. Sir, I need your agreement here and here."

The Congratulations Close

"I know it's a big investment, and you should congratulate yourself for being able to make an investment of this magnitude. You know, not everyone can even consider doing something like this. I need your OK here and here."

Do It Anyway Close

"You know, I understand it's more money than you had budgeted, do it anyway."

Money | Closes

The Disease Close

"I know it's more than you need and more than you wanted to spend, but look, it's not a disease. It's not like you're going to die from it. Let's do this, OK? Sign here."

The Inventory Close

"Where we move down or offer to move down a model. Would you consider this product, the product right underneath this? It would save you 500, 1,000, maybe $1,500. It will reduce your payments 12 to about 15 or $30 a month. Or, would you rather get exactly what you want and pay a little more each month?"

The Inventory Close-Move Up a Model

"OK. Hey before I write this up, I want to share with you that if we move up from the 4-gig to the 8-gig, or from the XL to the XLT, or from, you know, this neighborhood to this neighborhood, whatever the case is, when we move up a package, it would only be an added cost of X and with the payment programs in place, with the financing the way it is today, it would only change your payments a little, would you consider that?"

Money | Closes

Selection Alternative Close

"Hey, if the payments are too high, I suggest that we go back and consider the model I suggested earlier. It won't have the memory that you requested but it would put you in a position to get what you want and you can always come back and upgrade later."

Package Alternative Close

"Hey, if you don't want to go down a model, or consider something older, you don't want to consider something older, used, previously owned, why don't we consider moving down just the package. This would give you two options. It would first save X, it would reduce your payments by X, and still get you what you want. How about that?"

Money | Closes
Payment Breakdown Close

"OK? The payments are too high, I have to be under $500 or whatever the number is."

"John, we're already less than the 500 you want to pay. Let me explain it to you. Let's we're on an automobile. The car before options is 20,000 and that is a $400 payment. The GPS system that you want, the navigation system is $3000, that's $60 a month. The sunroof that you and your wife said you have to have is $20 a month, the leather 1800 that equates to $36 a month. The taxes paid to the state, the county and the, you know, the federal government which, hey, I wish you can get away with not paying them, or $60. The total is 576. Here are some options for you. Number one, remove the extras, OK? The GPS, the sunroof and the leather and the payments are $400 a month. Pay cash--Option two, pay cash for the equipment, keep all the equipment you want that your wife wants, the payments are 460. Option three, get the extras, keep your cash, pay the extra $3 a day and get exactly what you want. Look, I would personally go with option number three because you want to be under 500 a month, you already are, but it's up to you. Which one do you want to do?"

Money | Closes

Budget Close 1

"We're over budget now Grant."

Hey, everyone who buys from you is over budget, but we all still work it out. We have a support group here that meets on every Monday night just to--you know, just for people to gather and meet on being over budget. Look, I need your approval here, here, and here."

Budget Close 2

"And sir, you can probably say that about your credit cards, your car payments, your insurance, your taxes, groceries, restaurants, heating bill, your electric bill, they're all too much. They're all more than you want them to be but you still do them every month. Now, I need your OK here and here."

Money | Closes

Budget Close 3

"Hey, I understand that you're over budget, I understand it's more than you want to spend, and would expected this decision. We'll have plenty of company at home and it won't be by itself. And they say,'Oh, what are you talking about? What do you mean?'Look, what I'm saying is when you purchase today, it won't be the first time the first purchase that puts you in a situation that was too expensive and that puts you over budget. I need your OK here and here."

Budget Close 4

"So, assuming that you can afford your house, do this and afford your house, your present car note, your car insurance, your utilities, the gas, the water, the cable and the electricity, your groceries, your medical and your clothes, your baby sitter, school, entertainment, movies, restaurants, Visa and MasterCard, alimony, child support, your retirement contributions, health clubs, and you continue to save each month and would still have room left over for this purchase and enjoy owning this new purchase. Assuming that you could do all that, OK, then certainly you'd have no other reservations, right? Good. What is your house payment? What is your present card payment and you're going to go through the list."

Money | Closes

Budget Close 5

"Bar saying I'm over budget. So 90% of the people I work with are over budget when they get here. Just because you made some bad decisions in the past, OK, it maybe don't make sense to you today or purchase things then that really you didn't need should not mean that you would penalized yourself today for something—for getting something that you do need that does make sense and that you have to have at some point. Hey, let's do this."

Assume a zero balance

"Your payoff has nothing to do with the value of the product you're getting away. It could be a car, a boat or whatever they're trading in, OK? The value of it has nothing to do with what you owe. For instance, if you owed zero, would you want zero? Of course not they're going to say. Look, it's worth what it's worth, OK? It's not going to get any better by waiting. Pay the difference. If you can't pay it all, pay the difference and let's get you in this product now. Sign here and here."

Money | Closes

Down to the Penny Close

"Look, within $48.50 of getting you exactly what you want. In comparison to the price and the length of time that you're going to own this, that $48 is a minuscule amount. Let's do this."

Reduce to the ridiculous

"It's a thousand dollars a month. Look, that's $30 a day. You're going to live in this home, wake up in this home, go to sleep everyday in this home, you'll build your life here, your family here, create your security here, your future gets created for what, 30 bucks a day. You spend what, seven hours a day in your home or 10 hours or 12 hours, what is that, $3 an hour? Look, you can't rent a car for $40 a day. Let's do this."

Money | Closes

Can't Take It With You Close

"I agree it's a lot of money but you can't take it with you. Let's do this."

No Shortage of Money Close

"Hey I agree it's a lot of money but look there's no shortage of money on this planet. There is a shortage of people who are happy and who have love in their lives but there is no shortage of money. Let's do this."

Better to Live Rich Close

"Hey, it's better to live rich. You have payment or price objection. OK. Some kind of monetary objection and you're going to say, 'Better to pay a little extra and get what you want than pay a little less and make a mistake.' Better to live rich than to die rich. I need your OK here and here and I'll get your new product ready so you can start and enjoying it right now."

Money | Closes
The Justifier Close

"Hey how do you justify an investment of this size? See, this justify close can be used as the way to trial close or lock down a buyer. Where you have buyer close themselves by telling you how it makes sense. We talked about this in earlier segments where I'm like, look, get them to solve the problem. This should only be used for very professional closers that totally have their head on right who welcome knowing the truth of the matter and don't wish to cross their fingers and hope that deals get close but who actually want to close them. So what I might do in this situation is I'm presenting my product. I've done that. I'm sitting down, about to present my numbers. They've already somewhere in that presentation know how much money is involved. And then I'm going to ask them this question. 'Let me ask you, how do you guys as a company justify spending $3 million on investment like this? How would you make sense of it?' They're going to tell me, this close also eliminates any buyer remorse on the way out the door. It also allows the buyer to rationalize a decision for themselves which is critical for a buyer to make logic out of--at even the most emotional purchase, the buyer still has to be logical and make sense, justify it for themselves."

115

Money | Closes

Money Equal Close

"If the money was the same, which product would you rather own, or who would you rather do business with? Me or them? You got to get them to pick. Why them or why me, really why else. Why else until there's no answer."

It's Called the Treat Yourself Close

"Hey, of course it's a lot of money. And this isn't something you do everyday. Treat yourself to this. I need your OK here and here."

Work Hard to Earn This Close

"Hey, I know it's a lot of money and this is exactly why someone like you works so hard, so that you can earn the right to have those things that you want. I need your approval here and here."

You Deserve It Close

"I know it's a lot of money and you deserve it and if you don't deserve it, hey, I don't know anyone who does deserve it. I need your approval here and here."

116

Money | Closes

The Discount Close

"That's exactly the reason to do this now and get it for yourself so you can start enjoying it right now. I need your approval here, here and here."

No Equity Close

"Grant, I don't have any money at this time."

"So would you agree to owning your new product, this product assuming we can arrange financing with no money down out of your pocket? If so, I need your okay here and here that the figures are agreeable."

The Same Product Close (Yours)

"They say,'Hey, I've got a better price from a competitor.'Okay, which one and I appreciate you telling me that. Which one would you rather own if the money was the same?Oh, yours.' Why is that?'Well, because I like it better' and they tell you why. Why is that? And they tell you why. Why else? And they tell you more reasons. Why else? And they give me even more reasons. Then I say, hey, good, then you understand why we're more money. Now I need your approval here and here."

Money | Closes

The Same Product Close (Theirs)

"They have a better price from a competitor. You're going to say,'Okay, which one would you rather own if the money was the same? Which product would you rather own if the money was the same?' They're going to say theirs. Why is that? 'Oh, because I like it better, Grant.' Great, why is that?'Feels bigger, plusher' why else? Because it has this, this and this in it. Why else? 'Because they have something that yours doesn't have.' Great, follow me I want to show you something."

The Now and Later Close

"Number one, hey let me suggest that we show you the cost of doing it now and the cost of doing it later. Look, the cost of doing it now is $300,000. The cost later is approximately 6% more with the new price increases at the end of the year. This cost equals another $18,000 it's going to add $400 a month to your monthly payments not to mention that with this new product you, your company and your clients will benefit without paying the extra costs and benefit now. Look, you're going to do it now or you're going to do it later. I've given you the cost of doing it now and the cost of doing it later. The smart thing to do is to do it now. Sign here, please."

Money | Closes

The Gratitude Close

"Mr. Buyer, I agree it's a lot of money. Be grateful that you and your company are in a position to even consider this product. There are businesses that are shutting their door today and people don't even know where they are going to get their next meal from. They'd love to be in your position. You are able to own and enjoy your new whatever it is, you deserve it, you've worked hard for it, you're in a position to do it, be grateful you can. I need your approval here, here and here."

Who Taught You That Close?

"Buyer says 'We can't afford that.' You're going to say who taught you to say that? Who taught you to think like that? They're going to be like 'What are you talking about?' Sir, you can do anything you want and you can afford anything you want to afford. Look, that's not you saying that. I cannot even believe I'm hearing it. It's got to be somebody else, a mom, a dad, cousin, uncle, the newspaper, radio, TV, who is that? Hey, let's do this right now. You can do this."

Money | Closes

The Able Close

"Forgive me, please ma'am, forgive me, but when you say you can't do it today, I have to tell you that shocks me. You're one of the most competent, most able, most intelligent people that has ever sat in front of me, and I have people that don't have near your wherewithal who purchase this product every day. Now look let's do this. You know it's the right thing I need your signature here and here."

The Powerful Commission Close

"Mr. Johnson, any more of a discount at this point would result in me not getting paid on this transaction, and I don't believe that's what you want for me. What remains is the profit in this transaction is merely my commission and that is the sole and only way I get compensated and how I take care of my family. Come on, sir, come on, boss, help me out here. Look, I'm working day and night to take care of my family with only a small hope if I work hard enough I might get close to where you are someday. Sir, I need your approval right here."

Money | Closes

You Knew That Before Close

"I agree it's a lot of money and you knew that before you even got here. Look, I need your approval here and here."

Leave It Up to the Bank Close

"It's obvious you're concerned about the money. Let me suggest since money is the issue we leave it up to the bank. If the lender, the bank, the credit card, whoever is involved approves the deal and I know they won't approve it if they don't think you can do it, then we don't do the deal. If not, no harm done. Sign here, here and here and we'll leave it up to the lenders."

The Quality Close

"Hey, I know it's more money than you considered, and I would expect that this is the same thing that happens to you when you buy other products. It is obvious that you are a person who exemplifies quality, buys quality, lives in quality, wears quality and knows that quality goods cost more than other products. Look, let's get this done now so you can start enjoying the quality of this product."

121

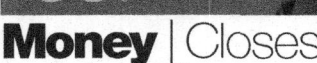

Money | Closes
Price Guarantee Close

"Hey since price is your only concern I'd like to offer you a price promise guarantee which is that if you were to leave here, okay, with our product and then later find a better price on the same product we will match that price or beat it. This is our way of giving you the assurance that you are getting the best price and you can make a decision now and do business with me. Since I only have now resolved your concern, okay, I need your approval here, here, and here.

Won't Be The Last Time Close

"I agree, and everyone that has ever bought this product said exactly the same thing. I need your approval here, here and here."

Payment | Closes

The Payments Are Too High

"Hey, compared to the payments of what? Come on, let's look at what else you're paying where you're spending the same or similar money and now getting nearly as much value."

"That's what you're hearing. Don't do anything about the payments. This is what you're going to do. Look, there's only way to reduce your payments sir. And I'd suggest what you do is take the balance, bring it down $2,000 by putting cash down. That will change your payments by about $44 a month. Shorten the term of the loan if you want to and keep the payments the same. Or look you keep your cash and you pay a little more money a month. Which one do you want to do?"

"I understand how you feel sir about the payments. Let me ask you, if these are too high how do you make sense of the ones you're making now? Look, you're paying too much right now for something you don't even want. Let's do this."

123

Payment | Closes

The Payments Are Too High

"Buyer just said Grant the payments are too high. But I know I'm on the right product. So it's better to live rich than die rich. Let's go ahead and do this even though the payments are a little more than you want them to be."

"Look, it's never too high for something you deserve. Now ask yourself, why do you work so hard anyway? Come on man, every day you go to work to grind it out. That's so you can do nice things. So what the payments are a little higher than you want them to be. Let's go ahead and get this done."

"Yes sir and compared to the enjoyment, the pride of owning the vehicle, the freedom from problems. And all the compliments you're sure to get. Look, the payments are not really a problem. Would it help if we set it up so you don't have the first one due for maybe a month?"

Payment | Closes

The Payments Are Too High

"Yes sir and the truth is you can't afford not to own this vehicle. Look, it's you. Let's figure out a way to make it affordable so that you feel good about it. For instance, if you put another $300 down it'll reduce those payments by about $6 a month, maybe $8. How would that fit? Well that's ridiculous. Exactly. Let's go ahead and do this."

"You're going to act surprised and say, you got to be kidding? You're shocking me. I'm surprised to hear that from you. You appear to be the type of person that could afford whatever they want when they want it. Come on, man. Let's do this."

"John, you can't afford to consider any other investment. Look, this makes such a powerful statement about yourself, your position, your success. So is it going to be in your name or your company's name? Let's get this done."

Payment | Closes
The Payments Are Too High

"I understand your concern sir. Look, I pay for things the same way everybody else, by the month. And if it's not in the budget, it's not in the budget. But let me ask you this? If you could pay all your bills, entertain yourself, tuck away money for savings and have enough money to pay for this purchase, would you own it? Once you get a yes then ask this question. Great, so how much is your rent, utilities, gas, food, credit cards, education, medical, recreation, savings, insurance? Make a list. You're looking for a surplus. And by the way, if you don't get a surplus don't assume that means you can't close this deal. You might still be able to close this deal."

Payment | Closes

The Payments Are Too High

"You must not be considering the savings just in maintenance and gasoline and insurance over what you're presently paying. Look, tell me, how much warranty do you left in your present vehicle? None? So any repairs are going to cost you out of pocket. Air condition $3,000, brakes, 1,200 bucks, okay, that comes straight out of your pocket. So what would you say it would be worth to you to know that your household and you and your budget is protected from any out of pocket maintenance expenses for the next three to five years? Come on man, this is the best investment you could possibly make in protecting yourself against those things."

Payment | Closes
The Payments Are Too High

"Let's look at some ways for you to make the car, the investment more affordable for you then. Look, let's remove all the additions, you know, a, b, c. Bring those additions together, take them off the purchase, save you about $88 a month. 'Oh Grant, I'd rather have it with it.' Good, let's do it. Lean on the pen. Let's roll."

"Forgive me but you pay more in property taxes, state, federal and city taxes every month than the cost of this. Let's get this done."

"So why don't you do this. Write me a check for the whole purchase, you won't have any payments at all."

"Great sir, and what reasons can you find for paying a little more a month than you wanted to? I mean, come on. Would it be the room, the styling, the comfort, the performance? The fact that you're protected financially? What would it be sir?"

Payment | Closes

The Payments Are Too High

"You just look at him and smile and say this. Sir, who's your insurance going to be with? He's like what do you mean? Who's your insurance going to be with? I want to transfer that over so you're protected when you leave here. Look, quit handling every objection. Discount it and close."

"So what I want you to do is this. When's your next payment due? On what you're driving now, when's it due. It's due in a week. Good, I want you to use that, actually write me a check for that today. We'll use on the new purchase and reduce your payments."

"And that John is more of a reason for making a decision right now. Look, waiting has already cost you too much money. Had you done this three months ago, your payments would be $20 less. Look, you're just making it worse by waiting. Can you see that? Good, let's get this done."

Product | Closes

Delivery Close

"When would you want to take delivery or have your new whatever installed? You want to do it right away? You want to do it tomorrow morning around 11, or a little later tomorrow afternoon? What would you rather do?"

The Check Closed

"Would there be any other changes, alterations or additions you'd want me to make to this proposal before we come to an agreement on the figures?"

Scale from 1 to 10 Close

"On a scale from 1 to 10 how would you rate your new purchase? Okay, good a 7. What would make it a 10? Oh, you'd have to do this, this, this, great let me get that handled for you, I'm going to get this, this, and this, I'm going to add that to our proposal, sign here and here and I'll get it approved."

Product | Closes

The Equipment Closed

"Hey, assuming we can get all the other items that you wanted, okay and have the product delivered as you've requested on your schedule. I need your approval here, here, here, and here, and also next to where I noted the changes that we want to add to make you happy."

The Title and Registration Close

"Hey, whose name will your new whatever be in, your name, your wife's name, the company's name, or all three?"

The Paperwork Close

"Whose name will we be doing the paperwork in? Your name? Your company's name or both names?"

The Insurance Close

"With whom will you be insuring your new purchase with? Great. What's their number there? I want to call and get coverage transferred so you're insured before you leave here."

Product | Closes

The No Other Reason Close

"If there aren't any other objections or reasons for not moving forward with your new purchase, I'll need your okay here, here, and right here."

The Momentum Close

"Look, I put all our numbers together for you, our best proposition. I can do this, this, this. We can do this. This is our delivery date. I need your approval here, here, and at the delivery date, and we'll get started right away."

The Re-Present Close also called The Redemonstration Close

"Hey, come see. In the close, come see, I want to show you how close we are to you making the wisest, most enjoyable investment of your lifetime. Follow me."

Product | Closes

Everything the same close

"Hey, if everything was the same, which product or which company would you rather buy from? Really? Why? Okay, why else? All right, why else?" Until there's no answer, and then you're going to go back through and use those to justify why you."

The Summary Close

"Henry, let me remind you of what you're getting here. You're getting the full library of training material. You're getting the complete audio version. You're getting the complete video version as well. You're getting workbooks for every one of your people. You're getting our 800 number for support. You'll have my cell number, my email and the ability to text me 24 hours a day and our staff. Look, man, I need your approval here, here, here, and here. Let's get this started."

133

Product | Closes

Comparison Investment Close

"Let's compare what you have now-- you're in the close, to what you're going to move up to. Here's the deal. Reality is your paying $2600 a month for your present situation, and you're going to move up to $5000 a month, okay? Let's take a logical look. Let's make this all logical on exactly what you're getting for the $2400. First of all, you're getting a better neighborhood. You're getting a safer neighborhood. You're getting a newer home. Writing this down. All new appliances, better resale value, a difference of what? $2400? $2400 divided by 30 is what? How much is that a day? I think it's $30 a day or $80 a day. $80 a day, and what are you getting? Bigger, better, safer, newer. Physically write each one of these down. Let's do this. It's worth the $80. I need your approval right here."

Stall | Closes

Spouse Stall Close I

"Hey what if your spouse says no? A, answer 'He won't say noGreat then I need your okay here and here. B, the other answer is more likely, 'Hey we wouldn't buy, if my husband says no or my wife says no we're not going to buy, you know, the product.You're going to say, 'Would he or she say now to the product or no to the money? If it's the product what do you suggest? If it's the money would it be the money, the down payment, the monthly payment, the price, all three, what would it be?' Once you work that out close the deal."

Spouse Stall Close II

"I agree, sir, and you should talk to your wife. But look. If your wife is anything like my wife, okay, she never tells me -- she never tells me no when it's something I absolutely have to have. When I've decided I love this, I have to have it, my wife always supports me and never tells me no, okay? Look. I need your approval here and here and right here. I believe your wife is just like mine."

Stall | Closes

Spouse Stall Close III

"Sir, it's better to ask for forgiveness than it is to ask for permission, so let's get going right away. I need your approval here and right here."

Spouse Stall Close IV

"Hey, I understand. And, if you and your spouse talk as much as me and my spouse do, then he or she knows, okay -- whatever the case is, they know you're here right now. And they know what you're doing right now. So look. Let's do this and get it done. If you don't have any other reservations, I need your approval here and here."

The Unavailable Party Close

"Okay, great. So the other person you need is not available, so let's write it up like this. You agree to ownership at figures and conditions spelled out. Delivery of the product, of the equipment, whatever, the service, is only subject to the third party's approval. Is that fair? I need your approval here and here."

Stall | Closes

The Unavailable Party Close II

"Hey, does your spouse or whoever the person is, does your spouse, in this case, approve of your present situation and the cost of it? Because if nothing changes, except for the fact that your situation is improved, certainly he or she would support you in improving your situation. Let's do this, assuming nothing changes, okay? If that's the case, I need your approval here and here."

Think About It Close I

"Grant, I need to think about.'

Sir, thought is instantaneous. I want you to think of an elephant. Did you get it? See, thought is immediate and instantaneous. It's not something that takes time. Think about the watch on my arm right now. How long did that take? It took that long. See, what I need you to do now is make a decision, not think about it. It's yes or no, now. It's do or don't do. Look, I'm fine with either one. Which one is it? Yea or nay? If it's yea, I need you to sign right here."

Stall | Closes

Think About It Close II

"Grant, I need to think about.'

"Hey, I understand you need to think about it. However, understand that thinking about it will not change the fact that this purchase saves you money, your company needs it and sooner or later, you're going to do it. Let's get it done now so you can think about all the other things that need your attention. I need your approval here and here."

Think About It Close III

"Great, do you think two or three days would be long enough or would two or three weeks be better?'Well, man, I don't even need two, I don't even need two or three days much less three weeksLook, the truth is no matter how long you take you're going to be faced with the same three questions either way. Could I share them with you? Number one, does this product get you what you want? Get an answer. Number two, can you afford this product? Get an answer. Number three, am I the person that you want to do business with and have support you in this purchase? If it's yes to all of them sign right here."

138

Stall | Closes

Think About It Close IV

"Hey, great. You know, most people want to take time to think about their decision before they make a decision. Let me ask you this. On a scale from one to ten, ten being you're absolutely certain and read to go, and number one being you wouldn't take it no matter what, okay? Where do you stand at this time on this purchase? From one to ten? Get an answer, okay? Then ask, no matter what he tells you, four, six, eight, I'm a nine, I'm a ten. Whatever he tells you short of ten actually, what would make it a ten?'Oh, well Grant, man, if you could do this, this, and this, that would take it from a seven to a ten, and I'd be ready to roll right now,' this is a great close, okay? Great close. On a scale from one to ten, where do you find yourself right now?"

Stall | Closes

Think About It Close V

"I understand you want to add some time to this and as a consumer myself, I have said exactly the same thing at exactly this time and here's the reality, when I was in that situation there was a couple things going on for me, okay, number one I was not yet on the right product and did not want to tell the sales person; number two, maybe the money was right, the terms weren't right, the condition wasn't right, and I didn't want to tell the salesperson or three, there was some other concerns that still hadn't been addressed. Let me ask you, which one's going on for you right now?"

Leave Me Some Paperwork Close

"The buyer says,'Hey, leave me some paperwork and I'll think about it.' Great sir, I'd be happy to do that for you if I thought that would help you. But I would expect a guy like you, that has six inches, maybe eight inches or 12 inches of paperwork on his desk right now. Look, let's make a decision on this. Get on with this so you can handle all the rest of the unfinished cycles, all the other things you have on your desk. I need your approval here and here."

Stall | Closes

I'm Going to Wait Close

"Certainly you can do that. Okay, you're in the close. The buyer says,'Look, we're going to wait a while.'Certainly you can do that. Let me just share with you what happens while you wait. Number one, you and your company still need the product. Number two, it's cost not to have the product. Just over the next three months it will cost you this. Number three, nothing changes when I leave here except prices possibly go up, you still need the products, you guys are still going to do this. Look, let's do this now and get it done. You have so many other things to put your attention on. John, I need your approval here, here and right here."

Stall | Closes
Nothing to Do with Decision Close

"Hey Grant we never make a rash decision you know. I need some time to think about it. Sir I hear you, and I agree with you, but look the reality is, there's only a few reasons, only a few reasons why you wouldn't do this tonight. None of which, by the way, has anything to do with your ability to make a decision. Can I share these with you? Yeah, sure what are they? One, lack of confidence in the product. Two, price or terms are not right for you. And three, you don't have confidence in me and the company. Now I want to know, which one is it?"

Stall | Closes

The Either Way Close

"We're not making a decision now. I understand sir. I understand mam. I understand completely. But the truth is, either way you're making a decision. Look you'll either make a decision to continue with what you have. Or you're going to make a decision to get what you deserve. Either way you're spending money. Either way you have an obligation. Either way it's going to cost you money. And either way, you've made a decision. The question now is, okay, whether you're going to reward yourself with something you need and want and will do anyway at some point in the future. Something you deserve. Or, will you make a decision to continue with something old, and that you don't want, you don't need, and no longer solves your problems?"

Stall | Closes

Rash Decision Close I

"We don't make rash decisions Grant. Hey, I understand and the reality is it would be impossible to consider any decision you make at this point a rash decision. Look you and I met on three different occasions already, okay, we spent probably what, 12-15 hours on this project? You, your staff, my people have spent hours considering the possibilities here doing discovery work, collecting data, doing due diligence, look you can't make a rash decision by saying yes now. Let's go ahead and get this done so we can get started."

Rash Decision Close II

"We never make a rash decision Grant." "Hey, I agree. And let me just say this, saying yes now could never be considered rash or a snap decision. Look, you've needed this product for years, okay. At this point not only would it not be considered rash, but doing it now is absolutely reasonable, logical and frankly the only thing you can afford to do. Look, I need your approval here, here, here and right here. Let's get this done."

144

Time | Closes

The Important Person Close

"Hey, due to your stature and influence in this town, we're going to do something for you we don't do for anyone else." Present the offer. "Sir, I need your okay here, here, here and right here."

Flush the Objection Close

"Hey, if everything were right, would you make a decision to purchase the product right now? You would? Good. So, what is it? The price, the financing, the product, the terms, is it me or the company? Write those five things down. Find out which one it is and wrap this deal up."

The First or Last Close

"Hey, look the reality is you're either going to buy this now or you're going to do it later. But you know you need this, and you know you're going to do it sooner or later. The question is do you want to be the first to do it or do you want to be the last to do it? Let's get this done. Let's do it and make you the first."

145

Time | Closes

Sooner or Later Close

"Look, the reality is you're going to do this sooner, or you're going to do it later, and you know it. You need the product. You've told you loved the product. You can afford the product. Hey, let's do this now sooner rather then later and get it handled."

Get It Done and Over Close

"Of course you could wait Mr. Johnson and not make a decision now, of course you could, but I want to get it done today so that you can put your attention on the other things that are more important to you and start enjoying the benefits now; sign here and here."

Never the Best Time Close

"Look, there's never a best time to make this decision as you will always have things going on. Let's do this now, get it handled for you and your company so you can start benefiting right now; sign here and here."

Time | Closes

Future Date Close

> "Look since I'm obviously unable to get you do this right now, can I at least get a commitment from you and an agreement from you that you will do this with me at some time in the future?"

The Now or Never Close

> "John this offer I'm making you is for right now, this moment in time; it's a now or never offer as will never be able to make this available and I won't be able to do it tonight, tomorrow, I can't even do it 2 hours from now. Because of the incentives we have available to us right now to hit our targets, I am not able to, okay, unfortunately I apologize but I'm not able and I want to tell you upfront, to offer you this after right now and I don't mean to put pressure on you, but it expires when you leave here; let's do this now, you know you want the product, you know it fits your needs, you're going to do it sooner or later, so you can take advantage of this incentive that we have this short window for. I need your approval right here."

Time | Closes
Get More Done Close

"Hey, look the sooner we get this done the more you're free to get the other things you need done and the more time you have to concentrate on all the other things not yet done. Let's do this now so you can get on with doing all the other things that require your attention. I need your approval here, here, and here."

Too Much Money | Closes
The price is too high

"Again, look even with that in mind, John, I assure you that your new purchase is going to prove to be the most enjoyable you have ever owned and the best investment you have ever made. Now when you want to take delivery?"

"Hey, and John, we have reasons for it being priced that way. Because of its limited production, high quality and tremendous high resale value, this investment will prove to be the least expensive of all like investments that you have made in the past. Let's do this."

"Look, it's just too much for your vehicle. So when you say the price is too high, do you mean the price of the new car, the value of your car, the difference, the payments or is a combination of all those things? You want to clarify here."

Too Much Money | Closes

The price is too high

"And you're going say, look, that's exactly why 95% of the people that buy this product have alternative ways of paying for it. What I mean by that is look, allow my bank representative tailor a payment plan you. Get you approved with one of our local lenders. Rates are at the lowest levels ever."

"You know, I'm not surprised you say that. What price was the vehicle that you're getting rid of today when it was brand new? How much was it? So your new vehicle is $4,000 more than the one you have now but it's 3 years newer, more equipment, four doors, not two, GPS system. You don't have that. Look, let's do this. You knew it was money when you got here."

"Hey, I appreciate the way you feel, sir. In fact, I have felt exactly the same way, and then I was made aware of why the price of the vehicle you have selected today is what it is. Can I share just a few of those reasons with you?"

Too Much Money | Closes

The price is too high

"John, we can easily adjust the price. Look, there's options on the car you selected that increase the price by this amount and pick that amount. However, if you can afford to go the extra 30 or 35 or whatever the number is per month, you probably deserve the extras. It's up to you. What do you think?"

"With the financing packages we have available today, I assure you that we will make this affordable. And if we can't, I wouldn't ask you to do business with us."

"Hey, I appreciate the way you feel, sir. In fact, I have felt exactly the same way, and then I was made aware of why the price of the vehicle you have selected today is what it is. Can I share just a few of those reasons with you?"

Too Much Money | Closes

The price is too high

"With the financing packages we have available today, I assure you that we will make this affordable. And if we can't, I wouldn't ask you to do business with us."

"Hey John, we have reasons for it being priced that way. Because of its limited production, high quality and tremendous high resale value, this investment will prove to be the least expensive of all like investments that you have made in the past. Let's do this."

"Hey John, I'll bet you have to say that about everything you ever buy. You know, it stands to reason that you would because everything you purchase you tend to gravitate toward the highest price, the highest quality because you have excellent taste for quality. Now let's do this."

Too Much Money | Closes

The price is too high

"Excellent sir. You know, the price properly reflects the performance and quality that will make enjoying the next four years of ownership even more so. Look, whose name is this going to be in? Your name and your company's name?"

"Hey and certainly John, you were aware of the price range of this purchase before you came down here. Look, you still decided to consider the product knowing it was more expensive. Now let's do this."

"And John, I would agree with almost anyone else. But knowing it is you that is saying that, what you demand from your investments, how you're going to use it. You know, how hard you work. The fact that you deserve the, this price of product, okay. Let's do this man. You know, you know you're going to end up in an expensive investment like this. I need your initials here, here and here."

Too Much Money | Closes

The price is too high

"What you're going to say here is this. Sir, it is too high, okay? It is expensive. It is a lot of money and be grateful that you're in a position to afford an investment in this price range and quality. Look, this wasn't built to be owned by masses of people, but people like yourself. Now I need your approval here and here."

"And John, I would agree with almost anyone else. But knowing it is you that is saying that, what you demand from your investments, how you're going to use it. You know, how hard you work. The fact that you deserve the, this price of product, okay. Let's do this man. You know, you know you're going to end up in an expensive investment like this. I need your initials here, here and here."

Too Much Money | Closes

The price is too high

"Sir, it is too high, okay? It is expensive. It is a lot of money and be grateful that you're in a position to afford an investment in this price range and quality. Look, this wasn't built to be owned by masses of people, but people like yourself. Now I need your approval here and here."

"So it's safe for me to assume that you have no other objections or reservations concerning the investment other than the price. Is that fair to say? You want to clarify right now and get your objections down to one or two things."

"Yes sir, I agree. And the quality of workmanship and unique styling do affect the price. And isn't quality and styling what you're looking for in your purchase. Look, I need your approval here, here, and here."

Too Much Money | Closes

The price is too high

"You heard that in the close again. You're going to say this. Have you ever considered the price of not owning a high quality investment product like this? Look, the cost of breakdowns that is not dependable, that it has poor performance, it has an embarrassing resale value, or even a trade-in when you go to get rid of it all go to increasing the cost of a cheaper model. Allow me to share with you or at least make a comparison of the cost of owning this new compared to what you're presently doing. I promise you I can make sense of this."

"It is high, sir. Look, I didn't pick it out, you did. And I offer to show other products that would save you money. And you declined. Let's do this."

"And Johnny, you won't be paying for the whole thing, either. Allow me to work it out, where you only pay for the portion of the car that you used and we'll let someone else pay for the rest. Let me explain to you what I mean. And then you're going to do your lease presentation."

Too Much Money | Closes

The price is too high

"And you're going to say, and with that price is included this company's superior commitment and my commitment to your continued happiness, satisfaction, peace of mind and the best service in follow-up anywhere, anytime, day or night, any time zone 24/7. Now, whose name will you be putting your name purchase in? Your name, your wife's name, the company's name, you tell me."

"Please forgive me, John, but I never do this but right now, I got to disagree with you. Look, when you take into consideration the standard equipment, the warrantee, the courtesy vehicle agreement that we have, the resell value and all the extras, OK? And when I'm paying for your vehicle, look, there is no better value on any other product in its class. Let's do this."

"Hey, I agree it cost a little more to own top of the line. Look, would you prefer to look at something else, personally? You look like the sort of person that deserves right of the top shelf. It's up to you. What do you think?"

Too Much Money | Closes
The price is too high

"And you're going to say, yes. The fact is you're investing in the most expensive automobile built on this planet and I can give you at least three important reasons for paying this price. Number one, you're getting the safest automobile that you can purchase in the world and I know that's important to you, would you agree? Number two, your new investment is more affordable, more comfortable to drive and will benefit you both in town and on the highway. You've already told me that was important. And number three, you're getting the best equipped, most luxury equipped automobile, uniquely styled car in today's marketplace. Let me add a fourth reason, most important. Look, you deserve it. You're a top-shelf guy. You're right off the top rack. Now, you think of four reasons not to own it, can you? Because if you can, don't do it. And if you can't, let's roll."

Too Much Money | Closes
The price is too high

"We're giving you a lot of these. You need to be, you know, long in closes. Look, allow me John to assure you. I can fix the price of any of our products, any of them. What I can't fix, what is it impossible for me to fix is your taste. It's obvious, you have excellent taste. Let's do this."

"Hey, you know, the truth is, it's the extra comforts that you've demanded from me that are causing the price to climb. Would you consider this same investment without some of those features? If not, I need your approval here, here, here, and here. Let's do this."

"And you're going to say, look, the price of this product is the number one reason for owning it. That's supported by every trade magazine written by the fact that the average number of days that this product sits in stock is under 10 days. Look, you deserve it. It's the right product for you. Let's do this."

Too Much Money | Closes
The price is too high

"You're going to say, hey, tell me, have you ever been in a position to look at or even consider this price product for yourself, anytime in your life. It's seems to me you've earned the right to invest in the most expensive, the most luxurious, and that thing which you most deserve. Let's do this."

"You could say, hey, great. Let's go back and consider a vehicle like this with low miles, a full written warranty, and save your self 800, 1200, $1500, maybe a little more. OK. This puts you in a position to break down those parameters in your negotiations. Use the alternative to cut your negotiations a price."

"John, the price everything these days, is too high. Look, leave it up to me to get the figures agreeable. Fair enough?"

"Lethal close. It's better to live rich than die rich. Let's do this."

Demonstration | Objections

I buy a car every year, I don't need to drive it or have time

"Well, great. I didn't ask you to drive it. Sit here as a passenger. Allow me to show you the unseen benefits of your new purchase."

"Look, I understand. I would not allow you to consider doing business with me if you're not completely educated about what you're getting for your money. It takes me 5 minutes. Bear with me."

"Look I understand you buy a car every year and I understand you don't need to drive it and I appreciate that. I assure you, however, there's been some changes that you are not familiar with. Watch this."

"Look, I know how valuable your time is. And I promise, I promise not to waste it. Allow me the courtesy of 5 minutes, and I'll show you something very, very important."

"Sir, if you determine that what I am about to show you becomes a waste of your time, I'll buy you and your wife lunch and make your first payment for you. Is that agreeable?"

General | Objections

Availability

"Greeting, incoming phone call even in a discussion when you're calling someone back maybe they ask they do you have any of And you're going to say this, don't say yes or no, say and how did you want that equipped as the answer. Once he tells you or she tells you exactly the way they want it equipped I want you transition to this question, you must be driving a vehicle like that now, I want to use that to qualify as a way of answering the original question."

"Grant do you have any of these?"

John we have the biggest allotment of those vehicles in the state and because of our purchasing power, because of our size, and because of our commitment to customers, no one, no one in the marketplace can sell that product cheaper than we can. Now tell me, how did you want it equipped?"

General | Objections

What's my car worth?

"You just got a phone call. Just had somebody walk in. This will work in either scenario.'Hey, what's my car worth?' Sir, what year is your vehicle? That is the way to answer that question. What year is the vehicle? Okay, good. Did you buy it new or used or as a demo? Okay? And what was the asking or list price at the time that you bought it? You'd want most of that back, wouldn't you? This is a great way to handle this customer."

"Phone call comes in, you pick it up and/or an internet request, or somebody walking in, 'Hey, what's that price? What can you do for me?' 'Sir, not only will I get you figures on that, I'd also like to get you figures on what you drove up in. Would that work for you?' You want to transition off the new onto what they're driving."

General | Objections
What's my car worth?

"Okay, in the greeting, on a phone call, hey not only when the buyer says,'How much? How much? How much?' 'Not only will I get you top dollar for the vehicle, okay, your vehicle, but I'm going to get you the best price on the new one, sir. Is that fair enough?"

"You're hearing this in the green, possibly on a phone call. 'Sir, I'd like to do that for you, as well as I'll get you a price on your vehicle, as well as a purchase price on what you want to replace it with. You know, what I'd like to do is show you both ways in case' -- 'What do you mean both ways, Grant?' Well, if you decide to keep your car and sell it yourself. I'd like to show you both ways in case you'd consider selling the car yourself and just getting a price on the new one outright. Would that work for you?"

General | Objections
I don't know what I want

"I understand. You know, with so many different products available, it can get confusing. Let me ask you this, to simplify. Do you want to go bigger or smaller than what you're driving now?"

"I understand. That's happens a lot. People come here, look around. They don't know what they want. I understand. Look, what vehicles have you seen that caught your attention and caused you to come here today?"

"If you did know what you wanted, you were completely clear on what you wanted, what do you think that would be? This will work more often than not."

"I understand. Let me ask you this, what is it you know for sure that you don't want? See you might want to start backwards here. Find out what they don't like, they don't want and you'll probably clarify what they do want."

"I just want to look around. Excellent. So let me ask you, John, what brought you out today to look around?"

General | Objections

Just give me your business card

"Hey, no problem sir. Here's my card. My name's Grant. Yours? John? Let me ask you, while you're looking, could I also get you information on your car?"

"No problem, sir. Here's my card. Surrender to that. Now, while you're looking, could I get you some figures on the vehicle you're interested in? Would that work for you?"

"Excellent, there's the card sir. If you have any questions could I follow along so I can assist you just in case any questions might pop up. I'll be right here. Just call my name. I'll be there for you."

General | Objections

How much money down?

"The best response I have is this. John, I'd like to show you with no money down today, would that work for you?"

"John, we have both lease and purchase programs right now with no money down. I can show you both ways and leave it up to you."

"You know, we have an ad right now with this amount down. It would create this monthly payment. How would that work for you? Buyer says, look, I don't have that much money down, and I cannot afford that payment. Great. Well, tell me what you do want, leave it up to me to get the money where you need it to be. Hey, if you can't buy here because of money it will be my fault, not yours. Get approval from management before using this one."

Greeting | Objections

What's your best price?
I got 10 minutes and I'm out of here

"Sir, 10 minutes, 10 minutes is more than enough time, in fact, in the next 10 minutes I'm going to get you the price you want, I'm going to get you down payments, I'm going to get you monthly payments and I'm going to get your vehicle fully appraised and top dollar for your vehicle. Is that fair enough?"

"Great sir, come inside and I'm going to get you all the information you need. Now when you go inside you're not going to start with the price. You're going start identifying exactly what these people want."

"Excellent sir and thank you for coming to our shop we appreciate you shopping with us for a price. Tell me how did you want equipped and I'll get you our very best price."

"Excellent sir, why don't I do this you have a business card or a phone, I'll get you the best price, I'll phone it to you, I'll fax it to you, I'll email it to you if that would be helpful in saving you time."

Greeting | Objections
I want your best price

"Great. When you leave here, John, I promise you you'll have the best price and enough information to make an intelligent comparison in case you want to shop. Now, how'd you want the vehicle equipped?"

"That's what you just heard. Super. Excellent, sir. That puts me in the best position in the marketplace to sell you a vehicle. Why's that? Because we can sell for less than anyone else in the marketplace. Hey, we're happy to get you our best price."

"That's the only reason we're here. Thank you, sir. Thank you for coming here to shop for price. We encourage you, this company encourages you, to make your final decision on price only."

Greeting | Objections
I belong to a Credit Union

"Excellent, great. Which credit union do you belong to? We do business with your members all the time. That's not a problem. We can handle it from here."

"Super, I love working with buyers who have enough information. You know, people that belong to Credit Unions have enough information and accurate information to make an intelligent decision. Great to have you here."

"Great, so you have gotten your financing in place, is that correct? Yes. Wonderful, you know we use your credit union as a source of financing all the time. What are they rates there now? Do you know? Good, just to keep in mind as an alternative we have a number of lenders that might actually be cheaper than your credit union. But we can worry about that later. Let's find something you want."

Greeting | Objections
I'm looking for someone else

"Excellent, super what kind of vehicle is your girlfriend driving now? Okay? Does she want to go bigger or smaller than that vehicle?"

"Excellent. And your name, sir? John? John, I'm Grant. Now what can I give you all the information on? If you're satisfied with it, then you can bring her back at a later date. Fair enough?"

"Okay, excellent! What is she driving now? Good, does she want to go bigger or smaller than that? What would you like to see her do? 'What do you mean?What would you like to see her do? You want to get him involved here."

"No problem, John. I work with people all the time who do exactly the same thing. Now let me ask you. What do I need to give you information on so you can bring that information back to them?"

Greeting | Objections

I know your cost.
How much over invoice?

"Sir, I'll work with you from pure cost. You make your decision on that alone. If the figures don't work, we don't expect you to do business here. Now, tell me, how would you like the vehicle equipped?"

"Excellent. Now, make your final decision on the money only. How do you want the vehicle equipped?"

"John, thank you for bringing the information necessary to make an intelligent decision. Tell me what you want and I'll work with you from our invoice."

"Sir, I've seen this dealership sell for less than $300 over depending on the programs and the product availability. Look let's find you a vehicle. I assure you money will not be the problem."

"What you're going to do here is this: Hey, thank you for the offer. The only thing more important to us than getting the money right is that we get the product right. Now, how did you want it equipped?"

Greeting | Objections
I'm just looking?

"John, my job is to give you all the time and information necessary so that when you do get around to making a decision, I'm confident you'll consider us. Fair enough?"

"Excellent, sir. My job is to find you the right product that fits your needs, fits your wants, and then provides you with figures you can agree with, even when you're just looking. Is that agreeable?"

"Excellent, and no problem. We'll give you all the time you need to look. Tell me, would you be looking at something bigger or smaller than what you own now?"

Greeting | Objections

I'm just looking?

"Great, great, we have an excellent selection of products for you to choose from. Now let me ask you, what are you most interested in looking at?"

"Let me know what you're looking for, and I'll point you in the right direction, so you don't waste any of your time."

"Then let me know what you're looking for and I will put some information together for you."

"That's why we display our products, sir, so people can come and look, ask questions and get the information they need. Where do you want to start looking?"

I'm just killing time?

"Hey, no problem, John. That's certainly allowable here. You can kill as much time as you want. Welcome."

"Sir, some of my best customers do that. My name is Grant. And yours?"

"So when you're more serious about doing something, sir, in the future, do you think you'll be going new or used?"

174

Greeting | Objections
What are the payments?

"Sir, it depends on what you put down and what your car is ultimately worth. But let me ask you this: what are your present payments? What does that matter? Because what I would like to do is show you how to keep your payments the same as the payment you're making now, or possibly reduce those. Would that work for you?"

"Sir, we have a sale on that car right now with a payment of, and give that number. How does that work? Oh, no, no. There's no way I could afford that. No problem. I can show you how to reduce that figure. Just let me know how you want it equipped, what you need on the vehicle and I'll work it out for you."

"Sir, why would you want to go with that vehicle? Did you know that you could go with this over here and save you $3,000, up to about $67 a month? All you're going to be giving up is this and this. It's a great car. It gives you everything this one does, but provides you with a savings."

Greeting | Objections
I'm not getting out of my car

"Hey, no problem. I would be happy to. Can I also give you figures on the vehicle you're sitting in right now?"

"Excellent, sir. The price of that vehicle is $26,800. Starts as low as $22,000. But let me ask you this, because it appears you're in a hurry. Any chance you would consider an alternative vehicle that would save you $1,000, $1,500, $2,000, maybe as much as $3,000? Okay? The alternative here is designed to get him out of his car."

"Excellent. Stay right there sir. Tell me, what do you want? Tell me how you want it equipped? Tell me any changes or additions you'd want to make. I'll hustle that for you right away. Oh, by the way my name's Grant and yours?"

"Excellent sir. And that's why we offer window service here. We do it all the time. If you'd like I could just have the information delivered to your office or your home so you don't have to sit out here in the heat or cold."

Write-Up | Objections

I want the bottom line.

"Look, there's nothing to go through, John. Let's go get you some figures. Let's go get your bottom line that you can agree to. Follow me."

"And John, that's exactly, exactly, what I want to do for you. Follow me and I'll get you the bottom line."

"That's what you just heard. Look, there's nothing to go through, John. Let's go get you some figures. Let's go get your bottom line that you can agree to. Follow me."

I've got bad credit or I went bankrupt.

"John, let me worry about that, okay? Promise you. I can still get you financing."

"John, I guarantee you -- I guarantee you -- we will get you financed. Okay? I'm the professional in that department. Follow me."

"John we get people financed all the time that had bankruptcies. That's not a big deal. Follow me."

Write-Up | Objections
I've got to go to my credit union

"When you talk to them they're going to want to know the serial number, product, how it's equipped. They're going to want to know the price. So what do you say we give you enough information so that you have enough information to actually assist them. Come on, follow me."

"John, we do business with every credit union in this state, and we do business with credit unions every day. You know, none of the other members -- by the way, what credit union do you belong to? He tells you. You know, none of the other members go there first. They actually get the information and deliver it online from here. Follow me."

"Hey, I don't want to go through all this stuff. I just want the bottom line."

"Look, there's nothing to go through, John. Let's go get you some figures. Let's go get your bottom line that you can agree to. Follow me."

Write-Up | Objections

I'm not buying today.

"That will be my fault, John, not yours. I take full and complete responsibility for your decision. Follow me."

"Hey, you always have the right to change your mind. Follow me."

"No problem. Let me give you some ideas of what it would cost you if you were going to buy today. That way at least you'll have the information.

Buyer puts a time condition.

"Hey, no problem. Let's go see what we can do for you anyway. Follow me."

"Hey, come on in anyway. You still need to have an idea of what it's going to cost you even if you're not making a decision today. Follow me."

"John, follow me. Under the right circumstances, look you won't have to wait until. Follow me."

Write-Up | Objections

I owe too much.

"John let me worry about that okay? Follow me."

"John, your payoff will not keep us from doing business. I promise you, okay? Follow me."

We gotta slow down here.

"Hey John, then let's slow down okay? And go inside and get you the information necessary so you have something to think about. And you have enough information so that you can make an intelligent decision. Follow me."

"Sir forgive me, I just thought that what we picked out for you was right for you and I thought you wanted me to show you what we could do for you with regards to the cost of it. Don't you want me to do that for you? Follow me."

"Hey, I didn't ask you to make a decision John. Only that we go in, get your figures so you know what it takes to own your new. Follow me."

Write-Up | Objections

We gotta slow down here.

"Hey, I understand you're in a hurry. Follow me."

"Hey, I understand, let's get you some figures you can agree with so don't have to spend any more of your valuable time doing this."

"Sir, let's go sit down. Let's get this done. Follow me."

I need to talk to my spouse.

"Hey, I appreciate that Jack and I would want my spouse involved too. Follow me."

"Excellent sir and no problem. Let's go get you some figures so you and your wife can have an intelligent conversation. Follow me."

"Hey so sir, don't make a decision today. Get yourself enough information and put yourself in a position where you have at least enough information so you know what your options are. Follow me."

Write-Up | Objections
I didn't bring my trade with me.

"Hey, no problem John, you don't need your car right now. Follow me."

"John, you don't need your trade until you and I come up with some figures that you like. Follow me."

"Hey so what? Let's go work some figures for you anyway. Look, don't let anything be a reason to stop."

"John, you don't need your car until you and I can come to an agreement about what your car is worth. Look, if we can't get to figures that you like, that you can agree to, you don't need to go get your car. Follow me."

Cold Call | Objections
Chapter 1
Not Interested

"Well, of course, you're not interested. You don't have enough information to be interested at this point. The reality is if you were interested, you would have called me. I wouldn't be calling you. Of course, you're not interested. You don't have enough information to be interested. The fact is you don't know me, and I don't know you. Why would you be interested? Wouldn't make any sense for you to be interested. Now, John told me to call you because, and he said to me, she's not going to be interested until she sees it. And, when she sees it, she's going to absolutely love this. Let me tell you what I do really quickly."

Cold Call | Objections

Chapter 2
I Am Busy / Don't Have Time

"I understand. I'm with you. And that's why I'm calling you. I understand you're busy, and that's why I'm calling you.

I know you're busy. I know you don't have time, and that's why I'm calling you today. And because you're busy and you don't have time, this never gets done.

I understand you're busy. I know you don't have time, and I appreciate that. Okay? When would be a good time? When would be a good time other than right now for you to give me 35 seconds? Literally 35 seconds is all I need."

Cold Call | Objections

Chapter 3
Send Me Some Information /
Email Me

"Hey, I'd be happy to send you over information. In fact, I have something ready for you to look at right now. What's your email?

Hey, let me text it over to you. I'm sending it over right now.

Excellent, I'd be happy to. In fact, I want to email it over to you or, better yet, text it to you right now, shows you what it is. I'll spend ten seconds going over with it. I'll spend ten seconds going over the information with you and you can see it, look at it."

Cold Call | Objections
Chapter 4
Not the Decision Maker

"Hey, great who would be involved in a decision of this magnitude?

Great, other than you, who would we be talking to?

Who would be involved other than you because I know you're important to the organization?

I know you're going to influence this in the right way. And oh by the way, who's that person? What's that person's position? And, hey what do you think is important to them?"

Cold Call | Objections
Chapter 5
No Budget

"Of course you don't have a budget for it. Why would you have a budget? Look, I didn't have a budget for Netflix before I bought it. I didn't have a budget for 99% of the things that I've purchased before I went out and put money down and said hey I'm going to do this. Look, assuming our solution actually could deliver you what I just told you it does, in fact let's just say it could only deliver half of what I just told you it could do and I could actually make this happen without any cost on your part, your company, your department, a division, literally it wouldn't cost you anything. Would you be the person to make a decision on this or would there be someone else involved?"

Cold Call | Objections
Chapter 6
Let Me Try It / Free Trial

"Oh yeah, I'd be happy to. And you know the reason people ask for trials is because they believe either they're not sure they're going to use the program or that the program is not going to work. Which one is it for you?

Look there's only two reasons you wouldn't do this today, only two reasons. Number one, you're not the decision-maker or number two you don't think you're going to use the program. And the only reason you would be concerned about using the program is because you've had other programs that failed you, that you didn't use. Look the truth is this, people buy bicycles, swimming pools and go to college and never use the information so I don't blame you for wanting a free trial. Well let me ask you right now what's your concern? Is it about the money or is it about the usage? Is it about you're not going to use it or it's not going to work? Or is it that you will not be the ultimate decision-maker?"

Cold Call | Objections

Chapter 7
Need to Talk to Director /
Executive / Board / Spouse

"Great! Oh super! Let me ask you something, okay. Who would that be, or with whom should I set that up?

Great, who would that be? Should I set them up with an executive summary?

Great, excellent! Who would that be? And, by the way, let's set them up, let's set them up with an executive summary. Let's set them up with something they can look at."you will not be the ultimate decision-maker?"

189

Cold Call | Objections

Chapter 8
Price Objection /
Too Much Money (In Greeting)

"Hey, I agree with you and based on the information you have right now any number, any number sir will be too much.

I am with you, A million, 3 million, 5 million, 50 grand, any number would be too much --, look, allow me to show you what I do. Put the money aside for a second, that is the easiest part of my job."

Cold Call | Objections
Chapter 9
Didn't Use the Last One We Bought

"There is a reason why people don't make decisions today and it's called uncertainty. Don't feel bad. People are not uncertain about their ability to pay for something, they are uncertain about their to actually use it. Is that your real concern?

Let me ask you when's the last time you bought something and didn't use it? Just because you didn't use the last one, does that mean that that'll be the case this time? Why would now be different now?

Tell me about a product you bought a long time ago and you still use it today. Tell me about one book you finished, one program you used. Let's focus on the ones you did use, not the ones your didn't, fair enough?

You've got 100 things you don't use right now. You've got a toilet in your house, are you using it right now? You've got a swimming pool at your house. You're not using that. What's the point? The point is when you're ready to use it, or you need it, you have it."

191

Cold Call | Objections
Chapter 10
Already Working
with Another Company

"Look, almost everyone I talked to today is already working with someone else... You have a need and right now, that company is fulfilling that need... or at least part of it. My goal in this call is to simply provide you with enough information so you can see that there might be a better alternative for you.

Look, I only need a few minutes of your time to see if this would even be a fit for you. The last thing I want to do is waste your time. If after a short conversation... I'm talking 60 seconds, if you don't see the value, if you don't see this is the best decision, if you don't see there's a reason to consider, the possibility of replacing them with me, then I'll hang up and I'll never call you again, fair enough?"

Cold Call | Objections

Chapter 11
What Do You Do?

"Hey, that's a great question, thanks for asking. We help companies (Fill in your big claim/value proposition, then move into your pitch).

Note: You need your big giant monster claim here. And you've got to concise, get your presentation right here to like a 15 second ad that you would invest money in on TV. "

Cold Call | Objections
Chapter 12
Call me Next Quarter

"Absolutely, I'd be happy to do that. Next quarter is great for us; in fact next quarter is better for me than right now. I'm going to send you over everything you need to know for next quarter, when are you thinking about in the next quarter by the way? Great, let me ask you what is one problem?

Note: you need to act right now like oh my God I'm so glad you're not buying. I am so overwhelmed with paperwork and contracts I thought you were going to say send me a proposal right now. Let them think for now that no is an acceptable thing... remember always agree. Lock the appointment then come back through looking for their (Dominant Buying Motive)."

Made in the USA
Coppell, TX
08 June 2024

33283544R00108